*50 College Admission Directors
Speak to Parents*

50 College Admission Directors Speak to Parents

Sandra F. MacGowan

Sarah M. McGinty

A Harvest/HBJ Original

HARCOURT BRACE JOVANOVICH, PUBLISHERS

San Diego   New York   London

Requests for permission to make copies of any part of the work should be mailed to: Permissions, Harcourt Brace Jovanovich, Publishers, Orlando, Florida 32887.

Library of Congress Cataloging-in-Publication Data

MacGowan, Sandra F.
  50 college admission directors speak to parents/Sandra F. MacGowan, Sarah M. McGinty.
    p.   cm.—(A Harvest/HBJ book)
  ISBN 0-15-601595-1 (pbk.)
  1. Universities and colleges—United States—Admission.
2. College, Choice of—United States.   I. McGinty, Sarah M.
II. Title.   III. Title: Fifty college admission directors speak to parents.
LB2351.2.M23   1988
378′.1056′0973—dc19   88-10918

Printed in the United States of America

Designed by G.B.D. Smith

First edition

A B C D E

To Barbara, John, and Jule

—S.F.M.

To my father

—S.M.M.

Acknowledgments

The field of college admission is a complex network—teachers, counselors, admission staff, alumni, testing services, federal agencies, parents, college administrators—all striving to ease and improve the process of education for young people. The admission professionals—especially the more than fifty here who became our collaborating colleagues—are a special group who impressed us with their concern for students. We acknowledge and thank them for their time, ideas, and writing talent. We also thank Elizabeth DeLaHunt, college counselor at the Latin School of Chicago, for being so very blunt and smart. Nor could we have completed the task without the assistance and tact of John McClintock, Nancy Donehower, Susan Moriarty, Marisa Casari, and Ellen Graham. Special thanks to our editors, Emily Thompson and Diane Sterling. And thanks and love to Linda, John, and Kim.

Contents

> *Susan P. Staggers, Dean of Admission and Financial Aid*
> *Mount Holyoke College*
> "We're just getting started on the college selection process
> with our teen and already we're in the middle of a family
> crisis. Are other parents having as difficult a time as we
> are?"

> *Robert H. Thornton, Director of Admission*
> *New College of the University of South Florida*
> "We haven't thought about college in twenty years! What
> should we do to help our child start choosing one?"

4

Contents

5

Testing: The Hard Numbers

Contents

Dona Schwab, Interim Acting Assistant Principal
Bronx High School of Science
A Guidance Counselor's View of SAT Coaching Courses:
Do They Pay Off?

7

The Competitive High School Record

Richard Steele, Director of Undergraduate Admission
Duke University
"Our child is not a straight A student. Just how important
are grades and how good do they have to be?"

Rae Lee Siporin, Director of Undergraduate Admission
University of California, Los Angeles
We Don't Need More Broccoli!

Lawrence A. Groves, Associate Dean of Admission
University of Virginia
"Our child went to a public high school. Do students from
private schools have an edge in the application process?"

Linda Davis Taylor, Dean of Admission
Amherst College
"How do highly selective colleges make their decisions
about applicants, and why do they seem at times unfair?"

Anthony R. Strickland, Associate Director of Admission
University of North Carolina at Chapel Hill
"How important are the recommendations of teachers and
counselors? Will they affect our child's chances of
acceptance at college?"

Philip F. Smith, Director of Admission
Williams College
"Does it help to send extra material with the college
application?"

8

William T. Conley, Director of Admission
Drew University
"Our daughter is ready to write college application essays but needs some basic advice on how to begin. Where should she start?"

Theodore O'Neill, Director of College Admission
University of Chicago
"Why do kids have to write application essays? Our son is going nuts—and so are we—trying to think of what famous person from history he'd like to have lunch with!"

Karl M. Furstenberg, Dean of Admission and Financial Aid
Wesleyan University
"Can the college application essay make a difference in our child's chances of acceptance?"

John Bunnell, Associate Dean of Admission
Stanford University
"We heard about a kid who got into Yale with an essay about socks lost in the dryer! Will only a high-risk essay get our teen into a highly selective school?"

Ten Common Essay Topics Colleges Pose

9

M. Beverly Morse, Associate Director of Admission
Kenyon College
"How can our daughter prepare for the college interview? She's very shy and needs some coaching."

10

The Financial Aid Hurdle   *177*

Special Schools and Programs for Special Students   *202*

12

Acceptance: The Moment of Decision

Contents

What to Do If Your Teen Doesn't Get in Anywhere

*Letitia W. Peterson, Associate Dean of Admission
Georgetown University*
"What do colleges look for in transfer applicants? Do
transfer applicants have a tougher time getting accepted
than freshman applicants?"

When Your Child's Favorite College Says No

13

After Acceptance: What Next?

*Susan H. Murphy, Dean of Admission and Financial Aid
Cornell University*
"Is there life after April 15? What does our child do now
that the waiting is over?"

*Michael Donahue, Associate Director of Admission
University of Michigan*
"Now that our child has been accepted, what can we do to
help ease the academic transition from high school to
college?"

*F. Sheppard Shanley, Senior Associate Director of Admission
Northwestern University*
"What social adjustments will our child face in college?"

*John W. Greene, M.D., Director of Student Health
Vanderbilt University*
"Our son is nervous about going to college. How can we
help him cope with college stress?"

14

Congratulations! Your Child Is Going to College

Parents' Questions Update

50 College Admission Directors
Speak to Parents

Dear Parents of
College-Bound Students

*"I was rather literary in college—one year I wrote
a series of very solemn and obvious editorials for the
Yale News—and now I am going to bring back all
such things into my life and become again . . . the
'well-rounded' man."*

—F. SCOTT FITZGERALD

Twenty years ago, if either of us had been asked why we chose our
undergraduate colleges, we might have said, "We didn't get in anywhere else!" Looking back, we both received some poor guidance
about choosing colleges. One of us did have the benefit of visiting
many colleges. Her father personally drove her to a dozen colleges,
and she was given the family car to visit other schools with two friends.
After serious investigation, she applied to three schools, without much
advice or support from her guidance counselor, and got these results:
wait-listed at an all-women's Ivy League college, wait-listed at an Ivy
League urban university, accepted at a highly selective liberal arts
college. Because her guidance counselor advised her that she would
never get off either wait list, she went to the liberal arts college. It

was an excellent school, but years later her choices seem to have been a bit limited. If she was wait-listed at two Ivy League colleges, there probably was another she should have been advised to apply to that would have accepted her strong high school record and combined verbal and math SAT score of 1410. She received a first-class education at the college she attended and went on to graduate school.

The other of us visited no colleges before she applied to the one home state university her parents said she should apply to. Their friends had a daughter who went to the state university, and her parents were intimidated by the prospect of investigating other schools and applying for financial aid. Of course, her A average and combined SAT score of 1304 made her a shoe-in at the state university, where, for more challenge, she found time to complete the requirements for two degrees in the four years it takes others to complete one. Had she been encouraged by her guidance counselor, she might have applied to other schools besides the state university. Nevertheless, she received an innovative education there in a newly formed writing option of the English department, and then she, too, went on to graduate school.

Our futures and careers developed as they did because we took advantage of opportunities presented to us, but both of us could have made more informed college choices had we received better advice. If you're on the brink of beginning the college selection process with your teen, you can recognize your own signs of "advice starvation" when—

☐ You plan to spend three hours a night for the next four months reading eighteen college guide books cover to cover—with a yellow highlighter.

☐ You skip the salmon mousse at the Reynolds' cocktail party for the chance to discuss the difference between "early decision" and "rolling admission" with a Princeton alumnus.

☐ You start wondering if hefty alumni contributions would have improved your child's application chances.

☐ You experience a strange queasiness in the pit of your stomach every time you wait at a traffic light behind a car with two college decals.

Sound advice is the key to getting through the college selection process with your teen. When we decided to write this book, we asked ourselves what parents might fantasize about doing to help their teens get into college—talk directly to college admission directors and ask them all the pressing, curious, silly, serious, demanding, even embarrassing questions they dreamt of asking about college selection. Because calling the admission directors of a few dozen colleges on the telephone is impractical, we came up with the next best thing— we asked fifty admission directors of colleges across the country to answer the questions on the minds of many parents we spoke to. Each gives a detailed answer to one of fifty different questions you and other parents have on your minds.

As you read the admission directors' advice, write down the questions that occur to you on the "Parents' Questions Update" at the back of the book. Then forward them to us. We hope to pass these questions on to other admission directors who will answer them in a future edition. If your first teen is college bound this year, these new queries may help your younger children when it's their turn to choose colleges. If you don't have younger college-bound children, the questions may help the people you know who do.

A word of caution: Discussions with your teen during these times can be nerve-racking. If a particular college admission director hits home about a problem you and your teen are having right now, give the director's article as a peace offering to your teen. Then pick up your heated conversation after you both have read the director's advice.

This book is for all parents of college-bound teenagers. We're on your side, and so are the college admission directors.

2

Grasping the World of College Admission

"Truth is never pure, and rarely simple."

—OSCAR WILDE

In the early 1950s, a young man applied to Carleton College, the alma mater of nearly everyone on his family tree. The college reviewed his record and suggested he come for an interview—to see the campus and to ask any questions he might have. His father wrote back: "Don't worry. I've told him everything he needs to know about Carleton already, and he'll see it when he gets there in September."

There have been radical changes in the college scene since Mark Rudd took over Columbia University's Low Library: in college costs, population, curricula, mores, and the role of the college *in loco parentis*. What colleges are, who's there, how to get in—and what to do once you do—have changed dramatically, and the situation for the young man who went to Carleton no longer applies. For many parents, helping a college-bound child is complicated by the need to unlearn old ideas and assumptions about college based on their own experience of twenty years before. In the gap between then and now, confusion abounds.

How exactly has the college application world changed? First of all, the process of choosing and applying is more complicated. In the past, except when special programs attracted them, most students looked at a handful of colleges and chose something nearby or at least within their geographic area; they took a set of tests and sent in a few applications. Today, students see themselves with a broader range of options. Our shrinking world makes Stanford seem reasonable to young people in New York. As a result, students now file between six and nine applications, with many filing twelve to fifteen, at colleges throughout the country.

Where the applications are going has created some changes, too. As in all aspects of American life, there are fads: certain colleges suddenly become popular. Schools familiar to parents may or may not "ring a bell" with this year's senior class. Even marketing experts aren't sure why some schools appear on every senior's list. Other popular selections are easier to explain. Prestige and the perception that certain colleges are sure pathways to wealth, success, and power have made a small handful of colleges desirable to many young people and their parents. The Ivy League (actually an athletic division created after the Second World War) includes schools that receive more than ten applications for every space in their freshman class.

Still, the enormous pressure to get into colleges has made college admission something of a business. As the competition has heated up, so each part of the application process has come under scrutiny. What can a parent do? The more than fifty admission directors you'll meet in the chapters that follow will answer that question for you. They will cover five strategic bases:

Planning and Choosing. Certainly, keeping up-to-date is the first step. Reading and researching alongside your child can make you both smarter consumers. College selection can be a bloody battlefield between parent and child as issues of independence and control are worked out, but clear and realistic goals can reduce the pressure and help you keep things in perspective. Don't expect too much of your child. Be realistic. Perhaps, after a little immersion in the business, the next step is a little distance, a little letting go. After you've read the first several chapters, you'll be convinced that most teens are happiest at the college they themselves have researched and chosen.

The most significant separation since kindergarten won't be painless for either you or your teen, but perhaps it can be less noisy.

Testing and the High School Record. College entrance test scores have held center stage for some time now, with plenty of controversy about their validity and uses. The proliferation of prep courses and books on "beating" the SAT suggest how intense this issue has become in the college selection process. But the real question is whether or not test scores are more important than the high school record in the final decision. If you think they are, the admission directors will quickly explain why they are not. They will explain, too, why your child doesn't have to get straight A's, or go to a private school, or spend his or her junior year behind the doors of an SAT coaching class to be accepted into a selective college.

The Essay and the Interview. Writing the application essay and preparing for the admission interview can both be traumatic experiences for a seventeen-year-old. If your ingenue is too eager, she may attempt a high-risk essay topic that could end up in the admission director's reject basket; if your leading man is shy, the only impression he may make at an interview is a dent in the chair he's trying to sink into. You'll hear seasoned advice from several admission directors on how your teen should approach the application essay and the admission interview. You'll also hear stories about other parents' teens that will help put your child at ease on paper and in conversation.

Financial Aid. It is probably news to no one that college costs have risen dramatically, with the average increase in tuition and fees at private colleges almost 150 percent in the past ten years. Parents need to begin planning early in order to cover costs often close to $70,000. The admission directors carefully explain how changes in government spending have reduced some loan and scholarship options, making financial aid a larger portion of most college budgets and at the same time a harder commodity to come by. What was once meant to provide the proper education for a clerical scholar is today a far more universal preparation for young people with various career plans and aspirations. In the face of rising college costs and U.S. Education Secretary William Bennett's complaints about "greedy colleges," many institutions must accept diminished public aid and find monies elsewhere. You'll learn how to plan for four years of undergraduate tuition and how to provide for several more years of higher education.

Deciding and After the Decision. Helping your child choose among the different kinds of admission and acceptance and then, finally, among several colleges is not as easy as most parents envision it will be. So much hangs in the balance. Looking at young people on campuses makes you wonder how many of their expectations have been met, how many disappointed, how many created at the college, how many discarded as unrealistic or no longer desirable. Like any relationship, the one between student and college takes time to develop—hence the many complaining letters and phone calls in the fall of the freshman year. Several admission directors will tell you that the students who hang on through the necessary adjustments find teachers, friends, and experiences that are stimulating and rewarding. Very few of these things could ever have been offered—marketed—to the student before his or her arrival. That's what makes the final choice so difficult.

How have things changed on the receiving end of all this intensity? Changes in admission office strategies have kept pace with changing trends among young people. The issues of selectivity have shifted, making some colleges nearly impossible to get into, others much more realistic choices than they might have been twenty years ago. In the competition with each other, college admission directors have hired market researchers, public relations firms, and image specialists to help them garner their share of this year's seniors. Direct mail is a part of the admission office strategy, and seniors literally receive boxes of mail from eager colleges. Admission office budgets have increased, marketing strategies have become more sophisticated, staff has been added, travel budgets have been expanded, and special programs in evenings, on Sundays, for counselors, for admitted students, for prospective students, for minority students have been worked into the calendar. Admission offices have computerized, enlisted students to help with the interview glut, and begun beating the bushes for students in untapped areas with high-cost videos and mailable cassettes. Some see the primary admission function now as recruitment rather than selection. There's a lot of punch and cookies out there for the taking.

"Hot" colleges and popular choices have skewed the selection function and created a buyer's market for young people at all but a handful of schools. Admission directors are working hard to keep the experience from becoming a revolving door for students. Their goal is not just to enroll students but to graduate them. What are the best indicators of "fit" between students and colleges? If personal qualities can predict success in college, how can applications accurately reflect such qualities? Admission directors continue to look for ways to check the validity of the selections they make.

As you experience the college selection process with your teen, remember that the most challenging part of the business is keeping your balance, avoiding the hype, and accepting the unknowable elements of the decision. Help follows: Admission directors have their say. You'll find out what's outmoded and what's new, what's useful and what isn't. Their advice will lead you and your child through the process, help you develop realistic goals, and bring you to April 15 with some appealing college choices. Fasten your seatbelts, sharpen those No. 2 pencils, and read on.

Getting Started on Choosing Colleges

"Nothing ever becomes real till it is experienced."

—JOHN KEATS

As we talked about writing this book, what bothered us most about the college admission process was the helplessness that students and their parents feel. Although the process is described as one of selection, the emphasis seems to be on colleges and their choice of students, not on students and their choice of colleges. Consider the following conversation with a young woman embarking on her senior year:

"I'm applying to Scripps, Smith, the University of Vermont, Boston University, and maybe Santa Cruz." Interesting choices, and a very interesting combination of schools.

"Why Scripps?"

"Well, I've been at a big anonymous public high school and I think I can do better and learn more if I study in an intimate and less distracting setting. I would like to get away from the East and into a school setting where I can be taken seriously for who I am."

"That sounds terrific, but where do UVM and BU fit into that scenario?"

"Oh well, for them I'm going to say, 'I've been in a really big, high-pressure eastern high school, and I know I can study and take advantage of the diversities of that kind of environment.' "

This young woman felt powerless in the college choice process. She was not choosing a school. Rather, she was bent on showing the colleges whatever personality she felt would please them. She was approaching her interviews with a gallery of personalities, one for every occasion. She had a sense of what she had to do to present herself as right for each school, but she had no sense of which school was right for her.

Certainly, it is difficult to know where to begin the college selection process. Students, on the one hand, usually buy a large pile of thick college guidebooks and sit on their beds, tuned to their Walkmans, highlighting in yellow the schools that sound interesting. They pay a lot of attention to what this year's senior class says and does, and they quickly connect to the schools that their friends tell them their brother's or sister's friends said were "great." Parents, on the other hand, usually talk to other parents, try to bring their own perceptions and college experiences up-to-date, read daunting articles in the local newspaper, remonstrate that "things sure have changed," and wonder how they're going to survive and celebrate their child's departure.

In general, both groups see themselves as powerless in the process, at the mercy of schools that will evaluate, weigh, and judge (and perhaps find wanting). They shouldn't. And neither should you or your teen. The selection process will be much less traumatic and, in the end, much more rewarding if you recognize from the outset the degree to which the choice is *yours*.

To help you get started, we asked admission directors in this section to speak to parents and their college-bound teenagers about beginning the admission process: what it is going to be like (and what it was like for one dean of admission with her own teenager), what the do's and don't's are, what role the student should play, and how parents can help without interfering.

Getting started here is like anything else. You have to give up waiting for it to happen to you and take charge. Forget the "right" answers. They're different for every applicant. And remember: The choice is yours and your child's. Encourage your child to invest in the choice, to take it seriously, to research it carefully. Selecting a college is one of the first adult choices of life. There are no right answers, perfect solutions, or clear-cut alternatives. Begin with compassion, support, and reasonable expectations.

MOUNT HOLYOKE COLLEGE

> "We're just getting started on the college selection process with our teen and already we're in the middle of a family crisis. Are other parents having as difficult a time as we are?"

Susan P. Staggers
Dean of Admission and Financial Aid

One might think that the son or daughter of a dean of admission would find the college selection process orderly and uneventful. To anyone else, our daughter Haviland, a junior in a private boarding school, had it made. I have sixteen years in college admission behind me, and her father has been involved with students on both the secondary and college levels for twenty years. Orderly and uneventful it might have been, but, in fact, nothing could be further from the truth. The reality is that my husband and I are as anxious as any other parents, and our daughter is just like other high school students who are concerned about where they will go to college.

It all started when the results of the Preliminary Scholastic Aptitude Test (PSAT) arrived in Haviland's school mailbox right after Thanksgiving. Devastated, she phoned us with the news: "With these scores, I'll never get in to College X or College Y. It was so embarrassing! Everybody was standing around the mailboxes asking each

12

other what their scores were. I didn't know what to say because the kids who were asking had scores in the 600s and 700s." Like so many of her peers, our daughter was mistakenly but inextricably tying her sense of self-worth to her test scores.

The next crisis occurred a short three weeks later. The minute she got in the car to come home from school for Christmas break, her father excitedly began peppering her with questions about colleges. When she had been home one day, I initiated a conversation about various colleges she might consider. We went to visit her grandparents during the school vacation, and even there any conversation with Haviland inevitably got around to where she was going to college.

Hindsight is marvelous, but that December my husband and I had very definite choices of colleges in mind for our daughter. These choices were based on reasons as vague as a good friend's daughter's having a fine experience at one college and a professional associate's assuring us that a young woman like Haviland would find College X perfectly to her liking. The facts that our friend's child was nothing like our daughter and that the "perfect fit" schools had virtually none of her sports interests registered only after prolonged and heated discussion.

We also had not realized how much our own egos were getting in the way of her choosing. It's not easy for parents, when asked where their child is considering attending college, to respond with the names of schools that produce a quizzical look and a comment like "That's nice. Where is it?" Parents want to invest, emotionally and financially, in a "name brand" for their children. How could our daughter possibly be thinking of a school that no one had ever heard of? The fact that no one we knew was willing to listen further to how marvelous an experience that college could be for her seemed to be a reason for lowering it on the list.

Haviland began talking about schools she had heard of from friends for what seemed to us to be the most superficial reasons. It drove us crazy. If we and others rejected her choices, then she would reject ours.

During the holidays, I insisted that she look through some objective college guides to get a rough estimate of the criteria she should be considering and that she write letters to schools that appealed to her. In response to Haviland's inquiries, letters and pamphlets began to arrive every day. Interestingly, the first letter she received came from a coach, although she had only mentioned that she played soccer and softball in an addendum to her letter. That the first communique to arrive was from a coach was reason enough for me to pooh-pooh the institution. My husband, however, was delighted—the university was "recruiting" her. Haviland, for her part, didn't know what to make of it because she had written to the admission office and not to the athletic department.

One can imagine what the holidays were like at our house: unending college talk came from every room. On her last day at home, Haviland and I were driving to the grocery store when she casually mentioned that she didn't think she wanted to go to college right after high school. Fortunately, I was only going 35 miles an hour when that pronouncement was made! As I white-knuckled the steering wheel and tried to make my voice as calm and even as possible, I asked, "What do you think you might do instead?" Her response was, "Well, I think I'd like to travel, maybe work in California, get an apartment, and take a few courses." We talked about other things for the rest of that brief trip.

When I reached home, I pulled my husband aside and we had a serious chat. It was at this point that we realized that we were a big part of the reason things seemed to be out of control. We had involved ourselves far too deeply and much too early with talk of college, and we came to realize that *we* were choosing a college for her based on what *we* wanted. We decided that a conscious effort to back off was in order. We restrained ourselves to the point of resolving not to bring up the subject until she was ready to discuss it. And we told her so. It was amazing how quickly this decision allowed all three of us to return to our usual good-natured bantering.

In March, Haviland brought home information from her "official" visit with her college advisor. There were a series of questions for students to ask about themselves and another series for them to ask about what they wanted in a college. For the first time, the three of us were able to have conversations about college that were not emotionally charged.

When we sat down together and acknowledged our individual expectations and Haviland's expectations, we became more realistic and more accepting of one another's opinions. In retrospect, it is easy to see that we had done exactly what so many other parents do: we had turned "college" into an emotionally loaded issue and unwittingly had placed an enormous amount of pressure on our daughter. Haviland's first visits to colleges during her spring vacation were made with her dad—and they both had a good time. Before she goes back to school in the fall as a senior, the three of us will be visiting another group of colleges.

So what was the result of all this? After I had written a rough draft of my article for this book, I showed it to Haviland and my husband at breakfast one morning. As they read, they both laughed. We knew then that once we had really started listening to one another, everything had begun to fall into place. Haviland will be going to college after high school. (She later confessed that she never intended not to go. She just wanted to see how I would react to the announcement.) She and we do not have any clear choices yet, but we are all doing our homework.

Mount Holyoke College is a four-year private liberal arts college for women, located in South Hadley, Massachusetts.

NEW COLLEGE OF THE UNIVERSITY OF SOUTH FLORIDA

> "We haven't thought about college
> in twenty years! What should we do
> to help our child start choosing one?"

Robert H. Thornton
Director of Admission

Earlier this year I received a telephone call from a concerned parent—a local influential stockbroker—asking my advice as an admission director about his son's application to college. "I'll do anything to get my son into Stanford—even cheat," the father said. "He deserves and will have only the best because he is my son." The parent did not stop there; he continued by asking my advice on how best to "guarantee" his son's admittance. He got my advice, but I assure you that it was not what he wished to hear. What I stated to him directly and what I humbly offer to all parents is my recommendation on what your role should and should not be in your child's application process to college, especially to a highly selective institution.

What I told this father was simple: Stop meddling and be honest! Give your child the essentials to grow and prosper and then leave him or her alone. In order to develop a sense of purpose, responsibility, and morality, a child needs help and guidance. However, this

16

help should not go so far as to include imposing your values. As your son or daughter approaches college, give your child solid suggestions about selecting high school courses (the strongest available in mathematics, science, English, foreign languages, and history), and respect his or her independence and initiative. This restrained help will lead to a better mind, more trust, and a refined sense of character. And to better college applications.

If you give respect, you will see a child with open eyes and diverse interests. If you demand and dictate, you will see a lack of commitment, limited self-expression, and inexperience. Emphasize personal happiness and fulfillment; do not focus simply on "winning" or on the "bottom line." Never overrate. Instead, give space, exercise your child's mind, note abilities, and encourage. In other words, treat your child as the adult he or she is becoming and as an adult likes to be treated.

On another level, don't equate the prestige of a college or university with its quality and appropriateness for your child. Only too often, I hear a mother or father saying, "This college is *very* selective, so it must be a good place for my child." It seems as though the more prestigious the institution, the more proudly the parents display the college sticker in their car's rear window, regardless of whether it is the best place for their child. Parents, you are the real perpetrators of this myth. Many of you do not consider what is ultimately most important: the academic and social happiness of your child. College is neither a badge to be worn at the office nor a financial and socioeconomic statement. College is the means toward your child's future happiness.

So what specifically should you do to help your son or daughter find the ideal college? Start early in the junior year to discuss college, but don't pick the subject apart. Speak consistently, loosely, and openly on the subject. Gear your conversations toward what your son or daughter needs from a college and *why*—city or country environment, fraternities or sororities, sports, student-to-faculty ratio, class size, special programs, and so on. As the year progresses, watch your child's growth. Speak frankly with the high school's college counselors. Ask them if other students have been accepted to the specific colleges that interest your child. What are the prospects for financial aid? Are there any particular deadlines to be met? As your search continues, listen to the information your child gathers, and pay particular attention to what attracts him or her to certain schools. Don't

17

forget to note well the successes and failures of those senior students whom you know. Remember that your child may be in the same position next year. See the problems, assess the stressful situations, and in advance openly discuss ways to address possible concerns for your child. Keep a calendar of college application due dates and deadlines, even though your child may change his or her mind about individual colleges. Throughout the senior year, be a part of your child's interaction with the high school college counselor or independent college consultant.

In keeping your child's options open, don't be unrealistic. Many students and parents are not pragmatic as they contemplate colleges. Each student should research options knowing whether or not his or her record is appropriate for a particular institution. You can obtain this information from college guidebooks, college placement officials, or school profiles. Remember, neither underrate nor overrate your child's chances of getting into a college. Be realistic.

And last, but a most basic point, don't type your child's application, write your child's application essay, or call the college to ask if your child's materials have been received. This is not your job! You are to *assist*, not *do*. By interfering, you make an admission director wonder about your child. Why isn't he or she calling? If your child cannot even complete the application without your help, how can I believe that he or she can do intensive, college-level work? I know that you pay the bills. I know, too, that you want the best for your child. And I believe parents when they tell me of their dreams that higher education will take their children up the mobility ladder. But you must understand that this process is stressful enough for your child without your demands and intrusions. Back off and allow your child a clean, clear, and concise effort of his or her own.

College today is not as it was in your day. Instead of imposing your past views of college, grow with your child as you both research tomorrow's options. College is a time to change, learn, and prepare for the future. It should be a precious and happy experience. You can make it so by concentrating on what will most please your son or daughter.

Good luck, and enjoy the start of a very worthwhile time with your child!

New College of the University of South Florida is a four-year public liberal arts college for men and women, located in Sarasota, Florida.

Help Your Child Deal with the Stress of Applying to College

Herbert F. Dalton, Jr.
Director of Enrollment Planning
Middlebury College

A troubling—and growing—component of applying to college is stress. Stress strikes both high school students and their parents. And in all too many cases, whether or not they admit it, parents are the source of anxiety.

Here are some reasons that parents can add to a student's stress and to their own:

☐ Parents may try to live their own lives through their children. One symptom of this syndrome is pronoun confusion, in which the parent explains to the college counselor, "*We* really want to go to Vassar."

☐ Some parents are unrealistic. They don't know their child's college admission "profile" (how he or she stacks up against other applicants) or how competitive certain colleges are. Much of their knowledge may be based on their own college admission experience and therefore may not be up-to-date or applicable to their child.

☐ For many parents, the college admission process represents the first time the child is in the driver's seat making decisions—which is also the last time parents are in control. Some of the parents' own unresolved feelings toward their child's new independence can infect the process.

As a parent, there are several things you can do to help your child cope with the stress of applying to college:

❏ Start talking about college with your child by asking questions. The family that begins the process by dealing with the question "Why college?" before trying to find the right college is going about things in the right order.

❏ Communicate. Listen to what is said or not said. Be aware of your child's concerns, priorities, and choices. Children, not parents, should fill out college applications and take the lead in the application process.

❏ Know the admission criteria for the colleges on your child's list and know your child's credentials. One unrealistic mother commented, "I knew Amy wasn't in the top 50 percent of her class, but I had no idea she was in the bottom half!"

❏ Help your child set himself or herself up for success. Make sure that your child applies to at least two colleges where he or she will be accepted. If you know your child can't get into Yale, don't insist that he or she apply.

❏ Let your child take the initiative. He or she should be the one scheduling visits and calling admission counselors with questions. If the child is responsible from the beginning, this can eliminate conflict down the road.

❏ A recent issue of *Spy* magazine listed the greatest fear of New Yorkers as "owning inferior children." Love your children for what they are and help them find a place where they can be happy and successful.

MACALESTER COLLEGE

> ### "We don't want our child to make a mistake in selecting a college. Where do students usually go wrong in the process?"

William M. Shain
Dean of Admission

Twenty-five years ago, when I graduated from secondary school, choosing a college was a relatively simple proposition. I visited half a dozen schools, all within two hundred miles of home, and paid little attention to the six pieces of unsolicited mail I received from other institutions of higher education. My idea of a thoughtful application strategy was to apply to three schools, all of them in the Ivy League.

The world has changed a lot in more than two decades, and the field of college admission certainly shows it. Students now begin thinking about college as early as junior high school, and I have even talked with parents of students as young as first grade! A student of any ability level can expect to receive enough promotional material from colleges to fill a few shopping bags. And the most selective institutions in the country are now twice as hard to get into as they were when I applied.

This situation puts a heavy burden on students choosing a college,

21

as well as on their families and on the colleges. Much of the resulting anxiety and intensity, however, can be eased if a student simply uses common sense. To help, I have assembled a list of mistakes I've seen students make in applying to colleges, along with ways to avoid these common errors. Share this list with your teen.

Don't attempt to change yourself to fit the college. First of all, the search for the perfect college must begin with the old adage "Know thyself." Too often, I see students trying to present themselves—or change themselves—to match a particular college or university. This posture strikes me as risky and even irrational. The point of choosing a college is to find an institution that meets your needs, rather than to sacrifice your sense of self on some institutional altar. The risk, of course, is that you end up at a college far less suited to your personality and learning needs than the school you might have found by a more thoughtful search process.

The best way to find this proverbial "fit" between student and institution is to present yourself as accurately as possible throughout the college admission process. This not only will enable an institution to get a better sense of whether or not you are likely to flourish on its campus but may even enhance your chances for admission. Back when I was a high school teacher, one overzealous parent completely rewrote her son's college application, including the essays. The result was a marvelously articulate and sophisticated presentation, with superb polish and tone. However, all of us who wrote recommendations for the student honestly described a candidate whose verbal abilities were ordinary but who had some special strengths: warmth, curiosity, creativity, and humor. These qualities were abundantly evident in the essay the student had written, but Mom had found the informality frightening and had vetoed it. The resulting hybridized file ended up faring less well than I would have predicted had the student done his own work.

Don't abandon common sense in investigating colleges. It is important that you use simple good sense in evaluating colleges and universities. Once you have set your personal criteria, your investigation should be active and should include a campus visit where possible. It is also important to remember that just as an applicant does not want to be evaluated solely on the basis of his or her SAT scores, so a college does not want to be evaluated solely on the basis of its students' average SAT scores. Actually, you should be careful about making distinctions between institutions with generally similar statistics, since no two institutions compute admission or other data in exactly the same way.

Don't let yourself be excessively influenced by college guidebooks. Good sense also dictates using some discretion with college guidebooks, which in general seem to range in value from the somewhat worthwhile to the downright misleading. Remember that few publications annually update all data for all institutions covered. Be skeptical of figures that seem unusual compared to those of other institutions, and inquire how the institution involved has computed, for example, a claim that 90 percent of each senior class goes on to graduate school. And, of course, although the guidebooks that evaluate colleges are often fun to read, they are also judgmental. Their conclusions may well be based on values other than your own. Just as you maintain a healthy skepticism about restaurant and movie reviews, remember that you should use your own judgment concerning reviews of educational institutions as well.

Don't spend too much time and effort in trying to gain a "competitive edge" in the college admission process. The onset of the college admission process shouldn't lead you to change your general approach to life. I find it distressing that so many students seem to mortgage their junior and senior years to getting into college. They attend counseling sessions and visit colleges, both good uses of their time. But they also take practice SATs repeatedly, spend huge amounts of their spare time on review courses of various sorts, and sometimes even work with independent college counselors when their own school already offers excellent college guidance. A heavy dose of these activities erodes the exuberance of the last two years of secondary school. Ironically, these activities may also indirectly reduce a student's chances of admission. Most selective institutions base their decisions on ratings that include both academic and extracurricular factors. Six to ten hours a week of college admission cramming takes time away from both course work and activities and can easily reduce a student's level of achievement in the very areas that colleges evaluate when making their admission decisions. And why live in a crisis mode for two years? If the same time and energy were devoted to traditional school activities, an application file might, in fact, become stronger.

Don't let the results of the college admission process affect your self-esteem. Retain your normal perspective about yourself and your world throughout the college admission process. In our admission office at Macalester, we try to use terms like *denial of admission* rather than *rejection*, since the latter term has emotional overtones that are not really appropriate to the decision we made. An admission decision is made on a *file*, not on a person. No admission process can accurately rank several thousand adolescents. Almost without exception, admission offices are populated by earnest, hardworking educators doing the best they can, but every office on occasion will underrate a student who ends up a Rhodes scholar somewhere else or will offer admission to a student whose years on campus turn out to be substandard in every respect. It seems both sane and healthy for students and their families to retain a mature perspective on what actually happens in the admission process, and not to take the results—positive or negative—too much to heart.

Don't compromise your integrity in your interactions with colleges. Most important of all, students and their families should hold fast at all times to their normally high standards of ethical behavior. This means that applications should be accurate in word *and* spirit. You should not apply to more than one early decision plan if each requires you to enroll if admitted. And since an enrollment deposit (or other type of matriculation commitment) is a binding promise to attend a college, it is unethical to promise to attend more than one college or university.

Finally, the best antidote to the anxieties of a college search is for families to function normally. The college admission process can be a largely enjoyable mutual endeavor. Campus visits, especially during the summer, can be interesting trips for the entire family, and you can profitably compare your perceptions of a campus with those of other family members. Several individuals working together can generate more and better questions to ask an admission officer—at a campus visit or in a letter—than can one person operating independently.

In general, I recommend that students and parents see college admission as an extension of normal living. Families should work together as they normally do, students should continue the school patterns that have always served them well, and most of all, families should evaluate institutions carefully through the filter of their own values. When a normal routine is combined with a thoughtful and persistent search for good information, the chances are pretty close to 100 percent that the entire college admission process will end well and be enjoyable along the way.

Macalester College is a four-year private liberal arts college for men and women, located in St. Paul, Minnesota.

One Admission Professional Reflects on Some Memorable College Applications

William C. Hiss
Dean of Admission and Financial Aid
Bates College

A week ago I was reading the application of a candidate from a liberal independent school in New York City when my eyes stopped and widened in amazement.

On the bottom of his relatively short list of extracurricular activities, he had neatly typed in "Primal Scream Therapy." He had checked off the appropriate number of boxes for his years of participation, and then in the space for "Positions, Honors, or Awards," he had typed in "Screamer."

The page of course went straight to my "blooper file," where I keep the startling announcement from a basketball coach that a candidate had "grown six feet in the last two years" and such unintended student gems as these: "I was abducted into the National Honor Society," "I proliferate with English courses and lust for geology," and "I function well as an individual or as a group."

But the next day brought a gentle comeuppance for me. Part of my laughter at this boy's expense had been at the unintended double entendre of *screamer*. In my adolescence and college years, this word had always been a slang term for a loud or obnoxious dunderhead. My young deans stared at me blankly when I told them this. The language, like a gentle mighty river, had carried me downstream into middle age without my quite noticing. It has probably been ten to fifteen years since I have heard *screamer* used that way.

But this student's application also made me think of the wonderful last minute of Woody Allen's great film *Annie Hall*. Looking at the camera, Allen says: "You know, there's this story about a guy who thought he was a chicken. People talked to his relatives and said, 'Well, why don't you get him into some therapy to help him get over this?' And they said, 'Well, we would, but we need the eggs.' "

The relationship between students and colleges is, in some playful sense, this kind of chicken-and-egg problem. Sure, we need the students and they need us, but not at the expense of their becoming neurotic authors of applications that make no sense.

I wish I could tell you that college applications never have the flavor of a desperate, absurd need to be loved. Happily, in most cases, the applications are good and helpful windows into young people's minds and energies.

TRINITY UNIVERSITY (TEXAS)

> "This is our first child to go through the college admission process. Could you give us a 'calendar' of how and when we should be involved?"

Alberta E. Meyer
Director of Admission

I have just come back from participating in our orientation for parents of incoming freshmen at Trinity University. It is always a wonderful event because the parents are excited and relieved that the admission process is finally over and their son or daughter has made the decision where to attend college for the next four years. In talking to them, I realized that this group of parents had been extremely involved during the entire process and intended to continue enjoying their son's or daughter's college experience. I asked them how they went about accomplishing this and the advice they would give to you as a parent who is struggling with your role in the college admission process. Here is what they said.

First, *believe you have a role!* Often parents try so hard to allow their child to make grown-up decisions that they stay out of the process. *Do not do this.* Think of yourself as a shepherd; you must guide and protect. Know your children and be tactful, but make sure you get some points across. This means you must do your homework so your advice is founded on the reality of today's college systems.

One parent who attended the freshman orientation told me about neighboring parents who wanted their son to learn a lesson in accepting responsibility. So they took a back seat in his college selection decisions and provided no help at all. After several months of floundering, the child missed crucial deadlines for the selective college that he had his heart set on, and he had to wait a full year before he could finally apply to that college again—this time on schedule.

If you are reading this as the parent of a senior who is investigating colleges, my next advice may be a bit late, but you can think of it as a checkup to see if you followed the right steps. I hope that during the time your son or daughter attended middle or junior high school, you worked closely with his or her counselor to select the appropriate curriculum. This is a very important step because it sets the stage for everything that will happen next. A solid academic program is important, and certainly a good performance in classes is equally important. You also need to encourage your child to think about developing some of the talents he or she inherited from you. Is your child athletic or musical? A natural-born joiner or leader? Look at what is offered in the school or in your community. I can hear you now saying that your son or daughter has done so much that your car is worn out from transporting him or her to soccer games, music lessons, and debating classes. It may have been rough, but it's going to pay off now that he or she is applying to colleges.

During the sophomore year, your son or daughter may have taken the Preliminary Scholastic Aptitude Test (PSAT). Your child probably got mail from colleges, and you realized that all of a sudden the college years weren't very far away. You also communicated with the teachers and counselor on the right curriculum, enriched or advanced placement courses, and the other things colleges would look for when they read your child's high school transcript. You had to do some convincing that extra work would pay off and not destroy your child's social life. You insisted that your child continue to participate in the music program, or audition for the school play, or—with an improved exercise program—try out for the varsity team. The bottom line is that you were involved in many decisions that were made during your child's high school years.

Early in the junior year, you checked to see if he or she again signed up for the PSAT and then, in the latter part of the year, for the SAT or ACT exams. You realized the importance of taking each test not just for practice but to see where your child stacked up against the national norm. These tests triggered still more mailings during the latter part of the junior year.

Your son or daughter began to get more mail than you did! Material from all sorts of colleges came in by the boxload and began to overwhelm your child. You helped to set up a system to sort through all the letters. You also discussed some of the characteristics your child wanted in a college: size, environment, location, programs of study. You encouraged your child to sort the brochures according to whether or not the colleges fit his or her needs. You let your child work through this process, but you also read some of the materials yourself and made helpful suggestions along the way.

While reading the college material, you began to notice something that all parents notice in college catalogs. You found yourself turning to the pages about costs. You had saved regularly from the moment your son or daughter was born, but you never really had an idea just how much a college education would cost over a four-year period. You did not want cost to play a major role at this point in the decision process, but you realized it couldn't be ignored, either. In the summer between the junior and the senior year, you planned your vacation around visiting colleges. Your son or daughter made appointments at each school and your family headed off. When the trip was over, your child finally had found the schools to which he or she wanted to apply.

Now your son or daughter is a senior. Encourage your child not to wait until the deadline to write college essays, but to begin drafting and writing them early. Your child will get a better chance if the application does not come in with hundreds of others at the last possible moment. Encourage your child to work closely with the high school counselor to ensure that everything is done correctly. Make a few phone calls just to be certain. File the financial aid forms that are required and check out all the other available resources. Look into any scholarships that might be available from organizations that you belong to. Encourage your child to call the college admission office if he or she has any last-minute questions.

Finally, responses will come in from the colleges to which your son or daughter has applied. Perhaps a positive response will come from a very selective school that might have seemed out of reach for your child, and a few other responses will arrive from schools your child was confident of being admitted to.

Be prepared to help your son or daughter deal with possible rejection from colleges, and convince your child that it is not the end of the world. Plan to sit down as a family to discuss what will be the final choice. This will be *your child's* four years, however. Remember, your child should make the final decision.

Another visit to the college campus may be necessary. But finally the choice will be made and your son or daughter will say, "Write the deposit check." Then just a few more things need to be done. You need to begin fading from the picture. If the college asks your son or daughter to write down his or her characteristics so that the housing staff can find a suitable roommate, resist the urge to put down "very tidy, goes to bed early, loves to study, does not like hard rock music at midnight." Let your child tell the truth.

The process is over and you realize that, as a family, you have done quite well. You now feel good about your son's or daughter's selection and—because you were involved throughout the process—you too are now planning to enjoy his or her college experience.

Trinity University is a four-year private university for men and women, located in San Antonio, Texas.

"What to Do When" College Calendar for Parents and Students

JUNIOR YEAR

Students

1. Think seriously about where you'd like to spend the four years after high school:
   - ❑ Ask three teachers you admire about their college experiences.
   - ❑ Browse through at least four college guides (some of the "numbers" variety and some of the "narrative" variety).
   - ❑ Talk to friends who plan to go to college and pay attention to what the seniors are doing.
   - ❑ Schedule a chat with your school counselor.
   - ❑ Try to figure out the kind of school setting in which you like to learn.

2. Take college entrance tests:
   - ❑ PSAT/NMSQT (Preliminary Scholastic Aptitude Test/ National Merit Scholarship Qualifying Test)
   - ❑ SAT (Scholastic Aptitude Test) or ACT (American College Testing Program Assessment)
   - ❑ Achievement Tests

Parents

1. Don't suggest possible schools until your teenager brings up the subject. Consider his or her choices first; then offer suggestions, *not* criticisms.

2. Remind your child that he or she can take some of these tests again senior year, if scores are low.

    ☐ Advanced Placement Examinations (where appropriate)

3. Write to colleges you are interested in or use the reply cards from the college mailings you receive to request:
   ☐ catalogs
   ☐ admission applications
   ☐ financial aid forms

4. Visit colleges during the summer:
   ☐ Keep a notebook of your impressions.
   ☐ Remember that you're only seeing architecture; you're not seeing the atmosphere when students are present.
   ☐ Schedule some interviews.
   ☐ Go back to teachers and counselors and ask questions.

3. *Don't* fill out forms or write letters for your son or daughter! Let your teenager do the job.

4. Spend some time on the campuses together with your teenager and then separate to allow your child to do more investigating alone. *Listen* to his or her impressions before offering yours.

SENIOR YEAR

Students

1. Talk to counselors about your final college choices:
   ☐ Explain *why* you're interested in these schools.
   ☐ Be open to their suggestions. (They know how students before you have fared at different schools.)
   ☐ Provide the guidance department with a final list of

Parents

1. Be patient as your child changes his or her mind several times before deciding on potential schools. Be realistic. Don't push your favorites too hard.

schools to which your records should be sent.

☐ Consider taking college entrance tests again.

2. Visit more colleges if possible, or return to two to four schools for a second look:

☐ See if your first impressions hold up when classes are in session.

☐ Narrow your list of potential colleges to about six you will apply to.

3. Ask two or three teachers to consider writing recommendations for you:

☐ Ask teachers who know you well and who will write positive letters about you.

☐ Talk to them about your goals and ambitions.

4. Fill out college applications, write college essays, and deliver forms for recommendations (with stamped envelopes) to your teachers:

☐ Show someone your essays after you write them.

☐ Proofread your typed essays three times.

☐ Stop in the guidance office and verify the schools to which transcripts, test scores, and letters are to be sent.

2. Talk to teachers about your child's college expectations. Be open to their suggestions.

3. Talk to counselors about your teen's college choices. Make sure at least a couple of choices are realistic possibilities.

4. Resist the temptation to write or edit your child's essay yourself.

5. Mail your applications early and relax, knowing you did a good job!

5. Remember that the transition from high school to college is a significant rite of passage to adulthood for your teen and a major change for you on the homefront. There'll be plenty of tension, so try to stay cool! Love your child and encourage him or her to have some fun before April 15—and to do some hard studying after!

Narrowing the Choices:
Reaches, Probables,
Safeties

"Look before you leap."

—JOHN HEYWOOD

As you and your teen plow through the mountains of information in guidebooks and in those daily deliveries of solicited and unsolicited mail, a little method can bring some order to the college selection madness. Once your teen has a sense of what he or she wants in a college, it should be possible to make a list of schools and, by their selectivity, create three categories: "reaches," "probables," and "safeties." Viewed as simple guides—not rules or absolutes—these categories can help a family focus realistically on what the applicant has to offer and what the college ought to be. The colleges choose in April, but some range of alternatives will provide your child with a choice, too, when the universal reply date (May 1) comes around. Here's how the three categories work.

First, the "reaches." These are the "dream" schools, the highly

35

selective colleges where the competition is breathtaking. Your teen may not have all the qualifications for these schools but he or she— or *you*—sure would like to go there. Perhaps the high school grade point average isn't quite as strong as it could be, or the transcript is a little light on advanced placement courses. Or maybe the SAT or ACT scores leave a few points to be desired. Nevertheless, applying to one or two of these schools can result in the surprise of acceptance.

After all, numbers aren't the whole picture. Colleges are looking for that elusive thing called "fit," and what they want is a strong but diverse freshman class, not a clump of clones. Don't push your teen to apply to colleges that are truly unrealistic, just on a chance. Any rejection is going to hurt. Don't urge your child to choose prestigious or popular institutions that don't really suit, either. One father told his son, "You can *go* to any college you want, but I will *pay* for you to go to Princeton." Parental pressure to apply to the top colleges can make young people feel that they have disappointed their parents. Some students act out their perceived inadequacies in their final semester at high school.

Dream schools should be more than dreams, appealing for something beyond their selectivity, exclusivity, and glamour. Your child should be knowledgeable about the reach schools and should have some possibility of acceptance. The guidance counselor is the best source of information here, as are records of how past applicants from your child's school have fared. Remember that the counselor has a good sense of both your teen's qualifications and the high school's track record at old Alma Mater University. It may hurt to see no Ivys on Junior's list, but restrain yourself from adding them if they're not reasonable reaches.

Next the "probables." These are the colleges where your teen has a good chance of acceptance. Again, the counselor and the high school's data, sometimes done as scattergrams to show what grade point averages or scores were accepted at individual colleges, are the best sources of information. Guidebooks, catalogs, and conversations with admission personnel can fill in the details. This is the most important category of colleges, and the bulk of your teen's applications should fall into it. All of these schools should be appealing possibilities. One way to create this list is to review the characteristics that made the reaches so enticing. As Kristin Crowley, college counselor at Horace Mann School says, "Examine the sought-after qualities and then find them elsewhere." Find similar characteristics in schools with student profiles that match your child's.

Finally, the "safeties." These should not be one or two guaranteed-to-get-into throwaways or "Mickey Mouse" colleges that seem to take everyone. Their selection is as important as, and perhaps more difficult than, the other colleges on the list. These are the schools at which your son or daughter has a strong possibility of acceptance. The rule for this group is: *Your child may enroll at one of these schools.* But the point is not getting accepted to a lot of places just for the ego of it. Sixteen invitations to the prom mean nothing if none are from the right heartthrob. Ask yourself and encourage your child to think, "What if this were the only college that accepted me?" Safeties may be the hardest to choose. One person's safety may be another person's reach, and no one can predict what the application pool at a certain college in a certain year is going to look like. Whether chosen for location, cost, or less competitive admission, these schools should also have as many of the desired characteristics of the dream schools as possible.

In this chapter, Douglas Paschall from Sewanee describes the choosing process as a journey. Rely on your counselor as a guide along the way. Gary Ripple talks about the role parents should play in the selection process. There's a fine line between support and overprotection. Duncan Murdock of Harvey Mudd College gives some practical advice about wading through the mailings. Remember, no college has pictures that aren't pretty! And Katharine Popenoe, from Princeton, discusses applying to the Ivys.

Narrowing the choices is probably the most important part of the college selection process. It takes time and research. It takes patience and understanding between parent and child. Some serious conversation with your child's counselor, a realistic vision of your child, and a strong resistance to the myth that highly selective schools take one or two "inexplicably unqualified" applicants are the best defenses against a disappointing April.

37

THE UNIVERSITY OF THE SOUTH

> **"Our son is obsessed with getting into one college. How can he be open-minded about other choices?"**

Douglas Paschall
Professor of English and Former Director of Admission

That students should have achieved the fullest possible understanding of themselves—of their deepest values and most cherished goals— *before* embarking on the search for college may be a worthy ideal. But the truth is that most students begin the process of college selection long before anything of the sort has taken place. Nor, let me hasten to add, is this a bad thing. Students who at age sixteen or seventeen know with positive certainty what they will be doing on a typical Wednesday morning some twenty years from now are in one respect as scary as they may be in others enviable. But for better and all too often for worse, college choices simply *do* reflect the deepest values and aspirations of students and their families. For this reason, as well as others worth considering, I believe it makes sense for the long and pressure-packed time of college search to be seen not as an obstacle to the process of self-discovery already in progress, but as an integral and potentially invaluable contribution to it.

38

My conviction emerges from the odd, if not quite unique, conjunction of nearly twenty years of teaching English in college and about half that long closely involved with college admission—including two different stints as director of college admission at Sewanee. You might think that these two involvements are, if not mutually exclusive, then at least mutually irrelevant, with the only possible link between recruiting and selecting students and a vocation in professing poetry as their occurrence within the same college.

However, the more time I have spent with prospective students—in on-campus interviews, conducting tours, talking to them after they have visited my classes as well as during school visits or over-the-table discussions at college fairs—the more I have seen that teaching poetry to undergraduates and advising students about their potential college choices have much in common, both in process and in ultimate purposes.

Among other things, a teacher of poetry invites students to make connections between a poet's concerns—emotional turbulence, complications among personal bonds, political views, beliefs about religious mystery—and their own. Like all genuine learning, a knowledge of poetry requires at least an initial motion outward from the self, away from self-absorption and our characteristic fascination with our own psyches (typical among adolescents, but scarcely limited to them!) and toward an acknowledgment of the separateness and dignity of creatures, utterances, and modes of existence not our own. Such an acknowledgment, if made with sufficient emotional and intellectual engagement, is bound to give us a fresh awareness of our own lives—of what matters to us, of what is most likely to contribute to our own and others' well-being, of what the world is really like and how it is best used and valued.

If most actual learning contributes at least something to the process of self-discovery that happens during school and college years, then why shouldn't the process of learning about colleges also make its own contribution? And if students and parents adopted such an attitude, what practical difference might it make to the pains and satisfactions of locating an "ideal" college?

One benefit would surely be a more relaxed approach to competing for places at so-called "prestige" colleges. For example, the worst effect of a student's obsession with gaining admission to one and only one institution is not that the student is being set up for disappointment and failure, but rather that the student will have far too early short-circuited the process of exploration and investigation—both of potential college choices and of his or her own needs and values. Thus the student will have abandoned or undermined precisely the goal of open-minded assessment of new possibilities that marks an educated person. Regardless of the eventual admission decision, the student who is obsessed from the start with only one college has already lost. By contrast, the student who takes a hard look at personal interests, abilities, and goals—who pursues clearheaded, open-minded research into several college options—has already achieved something eminently worth the effort. That such a student will almost certainly find a highly desirable college into the bargain comes almost as a bonus, though a well-deserved one.

Other practical benefits seem naturally to follow. Students conscious of the great number and variety of things about a college to be learned—about college curricula, laboratory facilities, library holdings and their accessibility, attitude of enrolled students, availability of academic and vocational counseling, even a college's assumptions about what constitutes an educated person (as reflected in its degree requirements and pedagogical habits)—are less likely to focus on a single personal shortcoming such as a mediocre SAT score or understandable insecurities like wondering whether anyone at the college will like them. They will make more and better comparisons of criteria that really matter to them. They will sharpen the type and quality of the questions they put to college admission officers. They will be less easily bowled over by something showy but specious in a tour or presentation, and better prepared to recognize what is valuable and significant. Their more inward and subjective sense of a college— their "hunch" about it—will seem more trustworthy. They will have made good *educational* uses of their college-search time. And they will have suffered far less of the helpless and unfocused anxiety, emotional distraction, and sense of powerlessness that typically accompany the college selection process.

As with many other significant choices in life, such as finding a compatible mate or a rewarding vocation, success is more likely to come as a consequence of a certain attitude toward the quest, of a secure sense of personal needs and values, than from a fixed choice or determination. Just as there are many potentially "ideal" mates or callings, so with the right sort of approach are there several "ideal" colleges. Managing to wind up at one ought to be the fortunate end of a process, or journey, that begins with learning as much as possible about oneself and the available options. The general goal is to embark on a lifelong process of *coming to know*. Although arriving at a suitable college is an important stopover during that process, both students and parents might remember that, more than any particular docking or mooring along the way, it's the journey itself that finally matters.

University of the South is a four-year private university for men and women, located in Sewanee, Tennessee.

COLLEGE OF WILLIAM AND MARY

> **"Our daughter says we're meddling with her college choices. How can we help without interfering?"**

G. Gary Ripple
Dean of Admission

Each chapter in the imaginary book *How to Be a Successful Parent* presents new and unique problems to frustrate even the most competent child raiser. Even if the parent is working with the second or third child, the problems are as dissimilar as the children. Such is the case with the college admission process. Parents have often told me that helping a college-bound teenager is perhaps the most difficult challenge they have ever faced. While their teenager is pondering the first major decision of his or her life, Mom and Dad are worrying about how much guidance they can and should provide. After all, college does signify a rite of passage. The child officially leaves the nest and sets off to seek his or her fortune. Selecting the right group of colleges and being admitted to the appropriate choice can be an excruciating experience for a teenager, and the teenager should approach the task with nothing less than great understanding, a significant block of time, and a thorough commitment to hard work. How many kids are so well equipped?

42

The changing relationship between parents and their children at this difficult time only confuses the issue and makes it difficult for even the most restrained parent to resist the protective urge. What if my child makes a bad choice? What if she misses the application deadline? What if he totally blows the SAT?

From my observations as an admission professional, even the most well-organized young person can suffer from an overload of anxiety during this trying period. Being able to demonstrate an understanding of the pressures a child is experiencing will enable a parent to be a soothing influence and a trusted source of support. Being able to overcome the protective urge and to encourage the child to set out on his or her own will only contribute to the trust necessary for parents to be an effective source of information and counsel for the college-bound child.

Instead of taking a back seat and providing help only when their child needs it, some parents try to take charge of their child's college selection. By making too many decisions and pushing too hard, these parents end up pressuring their college-bound student almost to the point of harrassment. This kind of unwanted help can have devastating results. I once received an application from a student who was so frustrated by her parents that she wrote at the end of the form, "Please don't admit me to your college. I'm only applying because my parents made me." I felt very sorry for this student and only hoped that she got to attend the college of *her* choice.

What then should be the parents' role in the college admission process? How much should you do and how much should the child be responsible for? Who should write to colleges for information? Who should call to make appointments for interviews? Who should fill out the application form? How much preparation is necessary to take the SAT? In my view, the applicant must assume a major share of the tasks of finding the right college and pursuing admission. Parents can be a vital part of the support network by giving their teenagers advice, preferably free of comments like "in my day" or "back when I was applying to college." But clearly, the role of parents in the college admission process should be as supporting characters rather than as main actors.

Today's vastly different college admission scene has evolved from a process that was relatively simple and uncomplicated just a few years ago. Faced with the sophisticated marketing plans of colleges and universities, the student must become an educated consumer of

43

higher education. Today's child is a lamb in the academic woods, where colleges are recruiting against each other as never before in the annals of American higher education.

Well-informed parents can provide support for their college-bound teenager in several valuable ways: (1) know the critical skills your child needs to make major decisions, (2) understand how he or she defines the important characteristics of the ideal college, and (3) help your child find specific institutions that meet his or her individual needs.

How selective colleges admit students is another important area for consideration. What standardized tests are required and how are they used? How does a student make a successful college visit and what are the fundamentals of a good personal interview? How should a student use college guidebooks and catalogs? What are colleges looking for on application essays? These are but a few of the questions that parents should know about and be able to answer to help their college-bound child.

The parent who knows when and how to step in with valuable advice can be a marvelous source of comfort and encouragement for a child facing the terribly complicated task of selecting the right college. Just as important as knowing when to intervene is the parent's willingness and ability to step back and allow the child to develop self-reliance. After all, once he or she is alone on a college campus, the child's self-reliance and self-confidence must carry the day.

With the pressures and anxieties that weigh so heavily on the situation, parents can and should become important members of the child's support network as the intricate puzzle of college selection and admission is solved. But the best way that parents can help their child is to realize that the college choice should be the child's own.

College of William and Mary is a four-year public university for men and women, located in Williamsburg, Virginia.

Guide to the Guides: Admission Directors Rate the College Guidebooks

A student once asked an admission interviewer why her college was a "two-telephone school." The interviewer was about to defend the technology of the school's switchboard system when she realized that the applicant was referring to a specific rating method used by a college guidebook to evaluate the social life at various colleges. The student's first choice was a "three-telephone school," and he was afraid he'd be unhappy at a school where the social life rated only two telephones.

Like the student in this story, many parents and their teens rely heavily on guidebooks as they develop their college choices. On the one hand, this practice seems perfectly natural. After all, we rely on guides to choose movies, restaurants, hotels, and automobiles. Why not colleges? On the other hand, it seems very risky indeed—a practice likely to produce satisfying results only when the personality, needs, and talents of the seventeen-year-old match those of the rater.

Before you and your teen decide to invest in one or more college guidebooks, you might want to consider a few of their merits and demerits. First of all, there are two basic types—the "objective" guides and the "subjective" guides. Encyclopedic in size and scope, the objective guides aim to be factual and comprehensive. Frankly selective and opinionated, the subjective guides aim to be readable and entertaining.

By reducing vast quantities of information about individual schools into manageable paragraphs and collecting it all into one volume, both types of guides can make the enormous task of selecting colleges less onerous. Certainly for statistics—enrollment figures, fees, housing facilities, male/female ratios, and the like—they can't be beat. Each type, however, has its pitfalls. On the one hand, the objective guides can be overwhelming; applicants can get so caught up in facts and figures that they forget about important matters like programs of study and methods of education. The subjective guides, on the other hand, can be oddly idiosyncratic, rating schools like olives, where *large* (read "competitive/selective") is the lowest grade.

Slavish adherence to any one guide, as in the telephone story, is dangerous. Guides are a good place to begin the selection process but not to end it. Both the numbers books and the narrative guides that purport to tell all (especially the secrets) are worth a glance, but be sure to supplement your reading by visiting campuses and conducting your own investigations.

Since most colleges object to being "cabin'd, cribb'd, confin'd" by reviewers, we thought it only fair to give them a chance to turn the tables. We asked the admission directors who contributed to this book to rate twelve popular college guidebooks. Most agreed to do so; ten did not. In the words of one abstainer, "The guides' ratings of us are misleading, so I won't muddy the layers of cocktail party chitchat by rating them in return. I prefer that students visit colleges and, with their families, make informed consumer judgments." We agree wholeheartedly. However, since guidebooks are clearly here to stay, we thought you might like to know which ones the admission directors think are best. The results of our survey are shown on the next page.

	INCLUSIVE	CURRENT	RELIABLE & OBJECTIVE	USEFUL
1. *The College Handbook* (The College Board)	excellent	excellent	excellent	excellent
2. *Comparative Guide to American Colleges* (J. Cass & M. Birnbaum, Harper & Row)	excellent	good	excellent	fair
3. *Peterson's Competitive Colleges* (Peterson's Guides)	good	excellent	good	excellent
4. *College Admissions Data Handbook* (L. Mazarri & L. Ekengren, eds., Orchard House)	fair	good	good	poor
5. *Profiles of American Colleges* (Barron's)	fair	fair	good	fair
6. *Lovejoy's College Guide* (Simon & Schuster)	fair	fair	good	fair
7. *Selective Guide to the Colleges* (E. Fiske, Times Books)	fair	good	poor	fair
8. *The Insider's Guide to Colleges* (Yale Daily News Staff, comps., St. Martin's)	fair	fair	good	fair
9. *Best Buys in College Education* (E. Fiske & J. Michalak, Times Books)	poor	poor	poor	poor
10. *Guide to the Best, Most Popular, and Most Exciting Colleges* (Barron's)	poor	poor	poor	poor
11. *Gourman Report* (J. Gourman, National Education Standards)	very poor	very poor	very poor	very poor
12. *Lisa Birnbach's College Book* (L. Birnbach, Ballantine)	very poor	very poor	very poor	very poor

KEY: excellent ◆◆◆◆   good ◆◆◆   fair ◆◆   poor ◆   very poor ◀

HARVEY MUDD COLLEGE

> **"Our child is inundated with mailings from colleges! How do we begin to read them, and are they all useful?"**

Duncan C. Murdoch
Dean of Admission and Financial Aid

"Hi, Dad. I'm home!"

"Hi, Perrin. How'd your day go?"

"Great! Got a B+ on my advanced placement 'lit' paper. Did I get any more mail?"

"Yeah, I'd say you did—about four or five pounds! I threw it in one of the boxes in the hallway."

"Which box, Dad?"

"The one by the stairway. I couldn't figure out your filing system."

"Way t'go, Dad. I had this all organized. The big box is for liberal arts colleges, the stereo box is for state schools, and the little box is for conservatories."

"What's this stack on the table?"

"Those are designer colleges, Dad."

"What's a designer college?"

"You know, everyone wears their sweatshirts with no intention of applying or the grades to get in."

And so it went—my family's first encounter with the daily barrage of slick, professionally produced brochures that Madison Avenue's advertising finest could be proud of. Of course as a dean of admission, I had inflicted my own direct-mail marketing campaign for years on every vulnerable high school senior who fit the criteria for our new freshman class. Now it was my turn to be on the receiving end. Not only did my daughter, Perrin, receive the slick full-color view books, catalogs, posters, and anything else that could be stuffed into a third-class envelope; she also received personal notes and phone calls from admission officers, students, and professors, and invitations to on-campus events, receptions, and auditions. A couple of colleges even sent video cassettes.

Discounting my parental pride, my daughter is a very good student, heavily involved in high school activities, and a great kid. But I must admit, she didn't exactly "blow away" the SAT, which made me wonder what kind of attention the really top kids were receiving. My guess is that between Ed McMahon's million-dollar sweepstakes, promos for time-share condos in Barstow, and college junk mail, most college-bound households need a shredding machine. I certainly don't remember getting this kind of attention. When I was in high school, the only kids who got any notice were a few academic superstars and a six-foot-ten-inch forward who could do everything with a basketball except *sign* it!

Today, if your teenager is in the top half of his or her high school class with average test scores, he or she is going to get mail by the pound from an assortment of colleges ranging from Dartmouth to Maxine's Institute for Diesel Truck Repair and the Culinary Arts. And if your college-bound youngster is a National Merit Scholar, plays the oboe, wants to major in chemistry, or is the leading spiker on the girl's volleyball team, you may never find your *National Geographic* in the mountains of mail.

Why the big change from when we were in school? The major cause is the increased competition for bodies brought on by the shortage of high school students. During the sixties and seventies, most colleges capitalized on the postwar baby boom and significantly expanded their enrollments. But with big enrollments came the need for more classrooms, faculty, dormitories—more of everything. In the late seventies, high school enrollments began falling (not something we didn't expect), and this trend will continue well into the mid-nineties. In some of the eastern and midwestern states the decline may reach 30 percent. The Sunbelt and western states will not be hit as hard. But the point is no one wants to have empty beds or classrooms, and no one wants to let faculty go. However, if colleges can't meet their enrollment targets, someone has to go—starting with the dean of admission. Get the picture?

The other reason for all those college mailings is that information technology has reached the college recruitment profession in a big, big way. Today's high school students can walk into their guidance office or "resource center" (years ago we called these libraries) and dial or punch in an "access code" (we called this a set of numbers) and presto—instant college catalogs and campus tours. Students can actually research hundreds of colleges on video cassettes, laser disks, and other high-tech media equipment. Many counseling offices have computer terminals linked to a data base that includes most of the country's four-year colleges. All a student has to do is choose the parameters he or she is looking for and enter those parameters into the system. The computer selects colleges that meet the desired features.

Let's say, for example, your teenager is interested in attending a small, liberal arts college somewhere in the Midwest and wants to major in chemistry. BLAP! Out comes a printout of fifty colleges meeting those criteria. Then your teen asks for a college with a varsity swimming team within a fifty-mile radius of a major city. BLAP! The list of choices drops to twenty. Now he or she asks for a college with a "Greek" system, selective admission standards, and an ROTC program, and the list drops to four colleges. Finally, your teen pushes another key and the computer generates a detailed profile of each institution, as well as the won-lost record of the lacrosse team and the hat size of the admission dean! The next step is to request information that may come in the form of slick full-color view books and catalogs, video cassettes (half of the households in the United States have VCRs), or floppy disks for those students who have access to a personal computer.

The fact of the matter is that students today can be far more scientific and global than we were about matching college choices to their needs. They are no longer restricted by not knowing what's beyond the boundaries of the state or region in which they live. If a student is looking for a medium-sized university on the East Coast with a mechanical engineering program, he or she may identify a couple of dozen to choose from. And if a student's college entrance test scores are above the minimum required by those colleges—look out! Those same two dozen colleges will be recruiting your youngster faster than it takes to compose a letter saying, "Dear Dean: Send me your catalog."

Just as students can run a profile check on the nation's colleges, so colleges can identify certain desirable characteristics in the student marketplace. We do this by buying into data banks of the College Board or the American College Testing Program. If your son or daughter took any standardized precollege test, he or she is in the system, and any college can tailor its mailings to students by location, ethnic group, grade point average, or test-score range. We can even determine if a student intends to major in a foreign language, history, or electrical engineering.

Back when we were in school, most admission deans were content to attract the majority of their freshmen from within a few hundred miles of the campus. If the college needed three hundred new freshmen each fall, it could meet that target by generating three thousand inquiries and six hundred applications. It wouldn't be unusual to offer admission to five hundred of those applicants to enroll a class of three hundred. That's a yield of 60 percent, which is unheard of in today's competitive market except for a handful (less than ten) of the superselective institutions.

Today the same dean may have to admit nine hundred students to make the three hundred target (a yield of 33 percent) and, to maintain any degree of selectivity, would need an application pool of at least fifteen hundred. This may require fifteen thousand inquiries— five times the inquiries it took in the sixties! Since there aren't enough potential students within our old market areas to generate those numbers, we have to look nationwide for qualified students. Why have the numbers changed so dramatically? Because in our generation students applied to only two or three colleges. Today on the average, they apply to three or four times that many. Naturally, this practice inflates our application figures to the point where all the selective colleges, and many that aren't selective, are experiencing record numbers of applications. The problem is that those records are being set by the same applicants at eight or nine other colleges. Our numbers are much softer now, and to offset our declining yields, we have to admit more freshmen. To maintain our selectivity, we need more qualified applicants, which means we all want more national identity. So we encourage more students to apply to more colleges—a Catch-22 situation.

Twenty years ago, the admission dean and a small staff would visit the high schools in the home state and perhaps the key cities in contiguous states. Now we have large, well-trained staffs and large budgets. Some of us even put full-time admission recruiters in the prime markets of California, Chicago, and the East Coast.

Back in the sixties, we'd get a call from a vice principal of a high school asking for someone from the college to attend the school's college night. "Sure, no problem!" Then we'd send someone from the English department along with a few catalogs and applications. These days there are thousands of college nights and scores of nationally organized metropolitan college fairs that may draw three hundred or more colleges and ten thousand students during a two-day period. And my guess is that the typical admission officer visits between 100 and 150 high schools each year. That's a lot of school visits for a staff of eight to ten people. We also talk of enrollment management, enrollment planning strategy, market share, imagery, market segmentation, forecasting, media coverage, secondary markets, market research, product design, and—of course—direct mail.

Years ago, with the help of the English department, we wrote and designed our own brochures. Today we hire consultants who specialize in college recruitment literature and designers who know what colors, graphics, and photos turn kids on. Our offices used to consist of two electric typewriters, three secretaries, and several color-coded three-by-five card files. Now we use scantrons, laser printers, computerized signature machines, and state-of-the-art word-processing equipment that produces letters so good you'd swear the head of the economics department sat down between classes to type them out personally. And these letters don't always come from the colleges you've never heard of. In fact, the more selective or prestigious a college, the more sophisticated its admission and marketing programs. The schools with the largest staffs and budgets are the "Ivys," the service academies, and the colleges that play football and basketball on national television. Much of the public believes that selective colleges don't have to recruit. That's nonsense. How do you think they become so selective? Ivy League colleges have been recruiting students for fifty years or more, if not with admission personnel and coaches, at least with a sophisticated network of aggressive alumni.

Now just because your teenager is getting mail by the pound doesn't mean that he or she will automatically be accepted to all the schools that have written. The information about your teen that colleges receive from the College Board and ACT is just a thumbprint. The admission application process asks for essays, teacher recommendations, and a complete transcript from the high school. Colleges may also require interviews, auditions, and art portfolios.

Here's how colleges use data banks of students' names for mailing: Let's say that College X gets the names of all potential social science majors with a B average or better (self-reported), a minimum SAT verbal score of 550, and a minimum SAT math score of 500. The college gets only the names of those students who score at or above those minimums; it does not get specific scores for each student, so it doesn't know who the perfect 800s are or who scored at the minimum. Of course, it may make sense for a college to search a little below its desired minimum to capture those students who have a big differential in verbal and math scores. If College X were an engineering college, for instance, it might wish to drop the verbal minimum so as not to eliminate the student with a 530 in verbal and an 800 in math. By the same token, it might want to raise the minimum math score. Typically, selective colleges like to see a balance between the verbal and math scores, but some colleges with special needs may drop either score just to capture a few of the extremes—high verbal and low math scores or high math and low verbal scores. Students with scores at or near *both* minimums may not be as competitive— unless, of course, they have very good grades or some exceptional talent.

So again, a word of caution: The information colleges get from data banks is, at best, a starting point for initiating contact with your teen. It doesn't tell us anything about what courses he or she has taken, whether the grades are going up or down, if your teen has built his or her own spaceship in the basement, or whether your teen was kicked out of an advanced placement English class for not reading *Moby Dick*.

Not getting mail from a college doesn't mean a school is not interested in your child. Rather, it may indicate that the college is so selective or so well known that it doesn't need to search for additional candidates outside of its primary market. It could also mean that the student's characteristics or desired major or region of the country is not a priority in the school's marketing strategies. For example, why should a West Coast university that is superselective in engineering send literature to potential engineering students in New England, an area with a high concentration of good engineering programs? It's not that the dean wouldn't like a top engineering student from the East; it's just that a direct-mail campaign to New England wouldn't be cost-effective because it would be too "low yield." On the other hand, if the chemistry or classical language department is hurting for students, the same school might be interested in New England students and might give additional incentives such as "no-need" scholarships. However, if you live in New England and you really want to attend a good West Coast engineering college, just write to or call the school. All of us love to get mail from students who take the initiative. In fact, that kind of student inquiry is usually more serious than the ones from students who fill in a postage-paid reply card and drop it in the mail.

Now that you've had a short course in college recruitment, what do you do about the onslaught of college mail presently filling your house? Some of it your teen should toss without reading; some of it he or she should glance at; and some of it your teen should read cover to cover. More than likely your son or daughter will apply to familiar colleges or to the ones you've been encouraging. But then every once in a while, a brochure shows up that just dares you to read it. It looks good, it says all the right things—it just plain fits! When that happens, I hope you won't discourage your teen from thoroughly investigating that college along with his or her other options. After all, at a time when most of us are afraid to be different and take chances, it's refreshing to see a seventeen-year-old break away from the traditional choices urged by family and friends. Besides, if we didn't attract a few students from other parts of the country who didn't know about us, we'd probably stop writing to them. And if we did that they might all just attend those colleges in their own backyard or the ones they'd already heard of—kind of like the sixties. What an interesting concept!

Have fun reading and good luck!

Harvey Mudd College is a four-year private college of engineering and science for men and women, located in Claremont, California.

PRINCETON UNIVERSITY

> ## "Should our son apply to all the Ivy League colleges and hope that one will accept him?"

Katharine S. Popenoe
Senior Admission Officer

It's safe to say that, in all but the most unusual situations, the "let's-run-it-up-the-eight-Ivy-League-flagpoles" approach to college admission is a poor one because it fails to take into account two significant variables: the individuality of your child and the particular characteristics of each college. There is no more important task in the college application process than exploring these two variables and finding the appropriate fit between them. The time and thought put into such an effort can be a positive, maturing, and confidence-building experience for your son or daughter.

In neglecting to make this effort, and applying more or less willy-nilly to all of the Ivy League colleges, you and your child may be left feeling that the college search process has been, at best, a distraction from the important business of the senior year and, at worst, a frustrating and possibly even destructive experience. Reasons behind such an approach are often misguided and have more to do with concern for prestige than with which type of school would be the most appropriate for a son or daughter. Families may not realize that the colleges termed "Ivy League"—Brown, Columbia, Cornell, Dartmouth, Harvard, the University of Pennsylvania, Princeton, and Yale—were originally grouped together merely as an athletic league and, in fact, differ from each other in numerous and significant ways.

As an example of unintended consequences, consider the case of Tom, a senior at a good suburban high school, who decided to take a flyer and apply to all the Ivys. His older sister had been admitted to an Ivy League college two years previously with a scholastic record similar to his but with outstanding extracurricular credentials—gymnastic laurels on a national level. Tom's high school guidance counselor cautioned that his academic and extracurricular record, though very good, would not stand out in the highly competitive Ivy applicant pools, but his parents saw the idea of applying as something of a lark and thought it might be his only chance of equaling his sister's accomplishment. Unfortunately, the following April brought eight thin envelopes with rejection letters from all the Ivys and an admit letter from an excellent college in one of the border states. Despite the letter of acceptance, Tom felt crushed and later told me, "I never realized what it would feel like to get those rejections and how much the time and thought I put into those Ivy applications had raised my expectations."

The psychological impact on Tom was considerable, ruining what should have been the triumphal final weeks of an excellent high school career of which both he and his parents had every right to be proud. Well into the first semester of his freshman year, Tom was in a state of depression, his confidence still not restored; he found it difficult to commit himself wholeheartedly to the social and intellectual opportunities his college offered in abundance. In retrospect, the "lark" seemed a serious and unfortunate miscalculation.

Parents, with the best intentions, are often behind the idea that a student should apply to all or most of the Ivys. They want the best for their children, and indeed, have sacrificed to give them all the advantages necessary to make them "college material." Parents may feel that, by matriculating at an Ivy College, their child will achieve prestige and somehow become one of the elite. One can announce with pride, "My daughter is at Dartmouth." Doors will open, opportunities will knock, admission to the right graduate school will be certain, and future income and status wil be assured. Although one must agree that prestige does count, it is well to remember that other factors are of equal or greater importance and that many non-Ivy colleges are highly prestigious.

Let's admit it, there are other motivations of which we may be only dimly aware, yet we should be honest with ourselves about them: the "right" college decal in the rear window of the family auto; the sheer exhilaration of living through our children's successes on the dinner-party or co-worker circuits; the gratifying possibility that our children may achieve many of the things we wanted but could not achieve for ourselves. The same strength of devotion that enables a parent to sit through twelve years of class plays, piano recitals, and losing soccer seasons can sometimes propel a parent to push blindly for what is seen as the most prestigious college, whether or not it's the appropriate choice for the applicant.

Parents and young people also may put emphasis on applying to Ivy League colleges out of simple ignorance of the tremendous array and variety of colleges in this country. Ernest L. Boyer, President of the Carnegie Foundation for the Advancement of Teaching, writes in *College: The Undergraduate Experience in America*:

> High school students and their parents may have strong feelings about college, but *choosing* one is a different matter. Indeed, one of the most disturbing findings of our study is that the path from school to higher education is poorly marked. Almost half the prospective college students we surveyed said that "trying to select a college is confusing because there is no sound basis for making a decision." Without adequate information, many students choose a college almost blindly. Then, once enrolled, they often are not satisfied with their decision and far too many, for the wrong reasons, transfer or drop out.

Simple brand-name recognition is not the wise or appropriate means of selecting colleges. Just as the list of the most admired men and women in the United States rarely corresponds with those *you* most admire, the most widely known colleges may not be the ones your son or daughter, if *well informed*, will most admire, want to be part of, and flourish within.

Beyond the obvious selectivity hurdle, and the high quality of their faculty and resources, all Ivys are not alike. To lump them together by applying to all of them is an indication of a lack of un-

57

derstanding of their profound differences. Among the ways in which the Ivys differ from each other are size, balance of graduate to undergraduate student bodies, dominance of professional schools, average class size, academic specialization, social arrangements, location, social ethos, and educational philosophy and tradition.

Furthermore, the attributes the Ivys share with each other are common to at least forty other colleges and universities judged by educational experts and reliable college guides to be "very highly selective" (as measured by scholastic potential, selectivity in admission, and quality of faculty and resources). Some of the most notable colleges are not Ivy League—colleges that exemplify and embody high ideals, exceptional educational programs, distinguished teaching faculties, and innovative curricula. Many have traditions and accomplishments the hallowed Ivys cannot lay claim to.

The Ivy League colleges often have more in common with other schools in the "selective" category than they do with each other, and you would be wise to make comparisons along these lines:

❑ Columbia has more in common with Barnard and the University of Chicago than with Dartmouth. The first three are located in intensely urban settings where the metropolis informs everything and "Greek" life is relatively unimportant. Dartmouth, on the other hand, is located in rural New Hampshire, and its twenty-three fraternities are considered by many to be a significant part of the school milieu.

❑ The general ambience of Dartmouth is much closer to that of its New England neighbor, Williams College, than to that of other Ivys. Location and ambience may strike you as relatively unimportant, but they are the most commonly cited reasons given by admitted students for choosing one college over another.

❑ In educational philosophy, Brown has more in common with Oberlin than with Princeton. Both Brown and Oberlin have liberal pass/fail options and emphasize freedom of choice and academic experimentation; neither imposes any distribution requirements. Princeton has both distribution and language requirements and permits no pass/fail option in courses in the major.

❑ Students interested in a career in government or politics

58

often apply both to Princeton, with its Woodrow Wilson School of Public and International Affairs, and to Georgetown, with its School of Foreign Service.

❏ Students interested in theater would do well to look at Northwestern University in addition to Yale.

People sometimes wonder if the Ivys divide and share good applicants. Considering the overabundance of qualified applicants for a limited number of spaces, do they try to avoid admitting the same candidates? In fact, the answer is no. These colleges generally are committed to a policy of admitting the best candidates in their applicant pools, even if they know, for example, that a student has been accepted earlier at another college. A candidate admitted to one Ivy school is likely to be admitted to more than one, and by the same token a candidate rejected by one may be rejected by all.

Of course there are exceptions. Recently a nationally known television personality told me, in the authoritative style that is his trademark, that applying to all the Ivy League colleges is exactly the sensible approach for applicants whose ambitions may exceed their accomplishments. His own daughter followed this course with truly dazzling results. Having applied to all eight Ivys plus Duke and the University of Virginia, she was rejected at all but one, Harvard/Radcliffe, generally conceded to be at the zenith of the selective college pecking order.

Proof positive that the buckshot method of applying to Ivy U. works after all? Or for that matter, that a famous name helps at a famous college? With either the innocence of the ignorant or the reticence of the proud parent, Dad had neglected to tell me what the decisive factor was in such a bizarre college application result. He is an alumnus of Harvard, which immediately put his daughter in a special pool of alumni children from which, compared to the applicant population at large, a significantly higher percentage are admitted. His daughter could have been spared the trouble of filling out many labor-intensive applications, as well as the slings and arrows of ten rejection letters, by a more informed and thoughtful approach.

This incident serves to illustrate one of the traps awaiting many an unsuspecting "college-headed" family. Rumors abound, and they are all too frequently based on half-truths and inaccuracies. Don't be seduced by them. Look instead to reliable sources, such as literature from colleges, comparative college guides, college counselors, and professors, undergraduates, and admission officers at the colleges your teen is thinking about.

The college search can and should be a maturing and well-supported first step into the adult world—a process that helps a student begin self-exploration at the same time that he or she investigates educational opportunities. To find the appropriate college "fit," a student must assume responsibility for information gathering, must assess his or her own strengths, and must learn to communicate these strengths to others. Doing this, in combination with clarifying needs and aspirations, is to begin to take control of and joy in one's own life decisions.

Several studies have found that parents are one of the two most important influences on a student's ultimate college choice (the other being the location of the college). Ideally, parents will aim for a middle-of-the-road attitude that supports but doesn't dominate their teenager's exploration—that encourages the student to aim high and take a shot at a "reach" or two but also to apply to several colleges that seem a comfortable bet for admission and to one or two "safeties," where admission seems certain. Parents will prove wise counsel for their chidren if they ensure that the "safety" has been just as well investigated, tested, and tasted as the "reach."

Students who take a major role in the college decision-making process will develop a commitment to their college choice that will do much for their success and happiness once enrolled. And, not surprisingly, students allowed to feel both supported and yet in control often wind up making the decision informed moms and dads would have them make.

Princeton University is a four-year private university for men and women, located in Princeton, New Jersey.

Calendar of College Application Deadlines

September Your teen should write for college applications this month. They aren't available any earlier.

October Help your teen schedule college interviews as he or she narrows the list of choices.

November The SAT is given the first Saturday in November (and other times throughout the academic year). The high school guidance office can supply dates. Encourage your teen to get plenty of sleep the night before.

Early decision application deadlines occur this month for many colleges. Check catalogs for specific dates.

December Your teen should spend this month polishing application essays for colleges with regular deadlines.

January Deadlines for applying to some selective colleges occur this month. Financial aid forms should be mailed after January 1, not before.

February Males over eighteen years of age must supply proof of draft registration to qualify for federal financial aid.

Some application deadlines occur this month as well.

March Your teen should arrange his or her list of colleges in order of priority and visit more campuses.

April Colleges notify applicants of admission status early this month.

May The first of this month is the "universal reply date"; a deposit check, with the intent to enroll, is due now. ▶

June   Wait-list action from most colleges concludes this month. If your teen has been wait-listed, you can wait for a decision, but you should have made a deposit somewhere else in May as well.

July   Orientation programs at some colleges are scheduled during the summer months.

August   Help your teen pack up and get ready to go!

Admission Committees:
The Inside Story

"We spend our midday sweat, our midnight oil;
We tire the night in thought, the day in toil."

—FRANCIS QUARLES

William Hiss at Bates College likens the candidate's vision of the admission committees that judge college applications to Dante's *Divine Comedy*: A stern judge waits to consign your child to paradise (admit), purgatory (wait-list), or hell (deny).

Who are these college admission people anyway? First of all, they are not the heartless judges of some apocalyptic vision looking for reasons to deny your child. Generally, admission people are hardworking individuals who want to do the best for their institution and for its students and faculty. They work long hours to create a strong, diverse, and interesting freshman class, and they strive for fairness and consistency. They are not a bunch of pipe-smoking, elbow-patched academics; neither are they a pack of number-crunchers or rah-rah alumni. In fact, the admission committees are different and distinctive according to their particular institutions.

Most colleges involve faculty in at least an advisory role, and it *is* possible that your teen's essay will be read by the chairman of the English department. Admission at Cal Tech, as Stirling Huntley explains, depends heavily on faculty. At Reed, Oberlin, and Sarah Lawrence, students are involved. Other colleges rely more on full-time admission professionals to make admission decisions. Most schools have a system that guarantees applicants more than one look, and you'll read about the typical route an application folder takes at a college. All schools use some form of committee to settle borderline cases of the type described by Larry Momo at Columbia University.

Whatever the titles of the admission personnel or the makeup of the committee, diversity of viewpoint is still guaranteed in the process. When students talk about "telling colleges what they want to hear," they are deluding themselves; they can't be sure of their audience in any kind of manipulative way. Among the ranks of admission professionals are recent alumni of the institutions they represent, seasoned staffers who have worked at several institutions, and senior people who have been at a single institution for ten or twenty years and may even have college-age children of their own. As Nancy Donehower at Reed and Leon Washington at Oberlin explain, there are plenty of different tastes, viewpoints, and priorities represented on any admission staff.

Despite their differences, admission professionals are committed to spending many hours in the dark days of winter reading folders, transcripts, letters, and essays. They view videos and slides, listen to tapes, and browse through portfolios. They code and mark and evaluate these items according to whatever system their school finds practical and efficient. Many schools use some sort of numerical coding to rate their applicants, and these codes are often unique to the school. You'll read about how the University of Texas at Austin uses computers to deal with the huge volume of applications it receives.

The business of the admission committee room is no mystery at all. There are no secrets about how to get into this or that college. Such myths are probably perpetuated by the difference between what admission people know about a single candidate and what you may know about that student if she or he has lived on your block for the last seventeen years. You've watched the child grow up alongside your own children; you know from your car pool that he or she got Austria and Australia confused until the sixth grade. Admission people don't have the advantage of such a complete view. Based on a thin folder of credentials, they must make a decision. If that decision inspires you to say, "I can't believe George got into Alma Mater University," that's all it takes to make the process of college admission seem like a whimsical, unpredictable business. But the judgments are meant to be reasonable, reliable, balanced; and where there are real points of confusion, admission officers pick up the phone and call the high school for clarification. There are sleepless nights on both sides—for parents and for admission people—but everyone works and hopes for the same ideal goal: fairness.

REED COLLEGE

**"Divine Providence or Dirty Harry?
Who makes those college admission
decisions anyway?"**

---

*Nancy Donehower
Assistant Dean of Admission*

The dream—now almost fifteen years old—remains clear in my mind.
I am transported, invisible, to the admission office at the college of
my choice. On a desk are half a dozen application folders. Somehow
I know these are the applications of the last six people to be admitted
to the college this year. With relief, I see my folder on top of the
pile. As I turn to leave, a man walks into the office. He is tall, dark
haired, grim looking. He is Clint Eastwood, dean of admission. As I
watch, Clint strides to the desk and picks up the top folder—*my*
folder—and considers it gravely. I stand, unseen and quaking, as he
utters the fateful words, "Do I need six students, or only five? In all
the confusion, I kinda lost count." Then, addressing my folder, he
continues, "So what you gotta ask yourself is, do ya feel lucky? Well,
do ya, punk?"

Even now, I shudder to recall that dream. The fact that I am now
on Clint's side of the desk makes no difference—I still break out in
a sweat. No matter that I have become one of the people making the
decision to accept or deny students' applications. My heart still beats

faster when I remember how terrified and powerless I felt as a seventeen-year-old waiting to hear from the college of my choice.

As I consider the admission process now, it seems unique. At no other life-changing decision point do you have so little contact with the person making the decision. When you take a job, you at least meet the people who will be your employers. When you get married, you are (one hopes!) intimately acquainted with the person who will share your life. However, when you apply to college, you often have little or no contact with the person or persons whose decision can have a profound impact on your life. A decision with very personal implications is being made in what seems to be a very impersonal way.

No wonder students feel powerless. The general lack of information about the admission process, coupled with the general anonymity of admission personnel, often leads to myth building and the construction of horror stories about those faceless folk who seem to guard the gates of higher education and hold the key to one's future happiness.

Working on the assumption that the truth can never be as horrifying as a product of your imagination, I would like to introduce you and your child to a few of the admission people I have met during my time in the field. Because I am concerned about the myths that have developed about the admission process and because I am tired of being perceived as Attila the Hun's first cousin, I want you to know that admission people are, by and large, an intelligent, concerned, humane bunch. By describing a few of my colleagues, I hope to dispel some of those monsters who gleefully consign applications to a dank, moldy dungeon of rejection or who capriciously admit a select few to educational nirvana. I'd like to give you a glimpse of the types of people who labor over your child's application.

When I became an admission officer, the first thing that struck me was the variety of people who had chosen to work in the field. There were young people fresh out of college who believed strongly in their alma maters and wanted to spread the word. There were older people who had master's or doctoral degrees, and people who had worked in such disparate fields as banking, law, teaching, and counseling. Some had trained for the ministry; others had been to medical school. One had worked as a backwoods river guide in a western state. Each one of these people brought different strengths and experiences to the job, but all of them came with a genuine liking and concern for young people and a desire to help them locate and take advantage of available postsecondary educational options. None was a ruthless, insensitive boor who took lightly the responsibilities of decision making.

To further illustrate this point, let me describe three of the admission people I have met during the past few years. I won't use their real names, but I hope the descriptions will reassure you and will help you understand that the people who read your applications aren't shriveled, humorless drones. On the contrary, they are people with quirks and habits, likes and dislikes, similar to your own.

❑ Joe has been in the admission field for about ten years now. He is married, with a family. He has a master's degree and has taught high school. Joe has a good sense of humor and jokingly says his military experience prepared him for the hardships of recruitment travel. At one point, Joe left the field and went to work in a bank, where he managed a sizable staff. He couldn't shake his commitment to education, though, so he returned to college admission work. He is an avid athlete, rarely seen without some piece of sports equipment, and he also loves to cook.

❑ Anna has spent four years in the field of college admission. Before that she lived abroad, completing a Ph.D. and teaching college students. She reads a lot and, some would say, indiscriminately: *Charlotte's Web*, *The World According to Garp*, *Psychoanalysis: The Impossible Profession*, and an issue or two of *People* magazine can be found in her briefcase at one time or another. She doesn't care much for sports but will walk somewhere when absolutely necessary.

❑ Dave is younger than the other two people I've mentioned. He started to work in college admission right after he graduated from college. He loves music and can sing an aria from *Aida* as easily as a tune by Talking Heads. He is always first in line to see a new foreign film, but for reasons known only to himself, he also goes to see films like *Return to Horror High*. He enjoys traveling and can be counted on to locate a good restaurant. Dave is also a big fan of roller coasters.

As I mentioned earlier, my purpose in describing these individuals is to help you realize that college admission people are a diverse, quirky bunch. It may help to keep this in mind as your child prepares his or her applications and writes those college essays. It is hard to write for a phantom audience and nerve-racking to try to guess what the admission officers will want to hear. Applicants will save themselves a lot of trouble if they avoid trying to homogenize themselves with opinions they think the faceless, mythic admission committee will favor. People like those I have described will be reading the applications, and, as the examples indicate, they have a wide range of interests. Perhaps knowing this will allow your child to feel more comfortable expressing his or her real self.

Perhaps, too, it will encourage your son or daughter to contact the admission people at the colleges that interest him or her. If your teen takes the available opportunities to meet and speak with the people who will be making the decision about the application, he or she stands a good chance of alleviating the feelings of dislocation and powerlessness that can accompany the submission of an application. And you and your teen may even sleep better, knowing that Clint Eastwood won't come anywhere near those application folders!

Reed College is a four-year private liberal arts college for men and women, located in Portland, Oregon.

CALIFORNIA INSTITUTE
OF TECHNOLOGY

> ## "Are college admission committees all alike? Should our child consider the committee's makeup when filling out an application?"

Stirling L. Huntley
Director of Admission

When an applicant's folder is assembled—test scores are reported, the transcript is received, the fee is paid—then the folder is considered complete and ready to be evaluated by the admission committee. But what—or who—exactly is the admission committee?

Admission committees at colleges and universities come in a variety of sizes and are set up in many different ways. Some colleges have no admission committee at all. The director or dean of admission reports directly to the college president or to a vice-president, and applications are evaluated by the admission office staff. Most commonly, however, colleges have an advisory committee on admission, which helps the director or dean of admission with policy matters or advises the president and senior administrators on admission policy. Such a committee might include faculty members, students or "senior interns," even alumni. This committee might suggest that the college look for a particular type of student—one with great breadth, for instance, or one with a narrow focus. It might recommend a balanced class or a class with strength in the arts or the sciences. It might advise stepping up the recruitment of minority students. It might urge that

70

fewer students with a certain specialty be admitted. Generally, these committees are not operational in nature but express the philosophy of the college on how the admission office should proceed.

Another common form of the admission committee is one that is largely advisory but also helps the admission office staff decide about difficult or sensitive applications. The admission committee members are invited to read a number of application folders each year so that they are familiar with the quality of the applicant pool and the nature of the decisions being made by the admission office staff.

The California Institute of Technology is unique in that all decisions concerning applicants are actually made by the admission committee. A few members of the Cal Tech Admission Office staff are members of the admission committee, but for the most part the admission committee is made up of active faculty members who take time out from their already busy schedules to read applicants' folders and to interview strong candidates throughout the country. After returning from these interviewing trips, the faculty members get together in small groups and admit the vast majority of the class. Then the admission committee meets as a whole to admit the last 5 to 20 percent. To my knowledge, no other institution has this degree of faculty involvement either in the interviewing process or in the actual decision making. Although it is a somewhat cumbersome and awkward procedure, it does assure the faculty that the freshman class will be a product of the faculty's own decisions. It also assures the institute as a whole that the applicants accepted will reflect the standards of those who will be working with them as enrolled students.

Regardless of the type of committee structure or the degree of involvement of the admission committee in the college admission operation, the best advice to any applicant is still the same: Be natural, express yourself honestly, and, above all, make sure to indicate all the activities that you've participated in so that you present as complete a picture of yourself as possible.

Students who know that their applications will be read by a faculty member rather than an admission staff person have no reason to distort their presentations. No matter what his or her position at the college, every reader who reviews the applications will be looking for the same qualities.

California Institute of Technology is a four-year private university for men and women, located in Pasadena, California.

Computer Admission at the University of Texas at Austin

Today, many large colleges use computers to help them with their admission process, from recruitment through enrollment. The University of Texas at Austin has one of the largest and most sophisticated admission computer systems in the country and uses an "automatic decision" process to handle most of its sixteen thousand applications each year. David Stones, data base coordinator for student affairs, explained to us how the process works.

As at other schools, UT buys computer tapes of the names of SAT and ACT test takers. It enters these names into its computer and then prints out a UT application form with the name and test scores of each student who has indicated an interest in UT. The already partially completed application is mailed to the student, who then returns it with his or her high school transcript. Based on entrance test scores and high school average, the UT computer automatically either admits or denies the candidate.

David Stones said that the UT computer can process more than seven thousand applications a night. He also said that students who fall into a gray area—those who cannot automatically be accepted or denied—are put into an admission review category and are asked to send recommendations to improve their chances for acceptance. Their application forms, high school transcripts, and recommendations are then reviewed by the UT Admission Committee, which includes admission staff and faculty members.

The system is both efficient and fair. It enables UT to process a tremendous number of applications each year, to give candidates a quick response about their admission status, and to review those applications that need special attention.

COLUMBIA UNIVERSITY

> "Not every college hopeful has perfect credentials. How do admission committees settle borderline application cases?"

Lawrence J. Momo
Associate Director of Admission

After nearly fifteen years in the admission business, I continue to be struck by the seeming unfairness of its timetable. Applicants are asked to submit by January 1 extensive dossiers about themselves—a four-page application with essay(s); transcripts of their academic performance; recommendations from teachers, counselors, and others with whom they have worked; evidence of special talent or achievement; an interview—and then they are asked to wait and wait and wait until the middle of April when the mail arrives bringing news of elation, disappointment, or perhaps still further waiting. What is it that goes on during that time of near-interminable silence? How is it that a class is selected anyway? Which factors make a difference when the decisions are fine-tuned? How can you keep it all in perspective? Let me see if I can't shed some light on these mysteries.

Much of what I say here pertains specifically to Columbia, of course, and only by extension to other schools. I hope my colleagues will agree, though, that their processes are a variation of this one. The time between January and April is spent quietly reading and at times heatedly discussing cases. The process of selection is one in which a great deal of care and effort is invested. Once a file is complete, meaning that the various parts of the application have been received, it is read first by the admission professional on our staff who is responsible for the geographic area from which that application originated. "Reading a file" in our parlance means evaluating the candidate both academically and personally on a rating scale of 1 to 5, 5 being the highest. An academic appraisal is our estimate of an individual's ability to do the work here at Columbia. It is based on an applicant's performance in high school—grades, rank in class, and curriculum difficulty—along with standardized test scores and recommendations from teachers and counselors as they touch on academic matters. The personal evaluation is somewhat more subtle and concerns itself with who someone is as evinced by what he or she does outside of class. It includes school involvement, to be sure, but it also includes out-of-school activities: hobbies pursued, special talents demonstrated, community service performed, jobs held, and travel experiences enjoyed. Once an applicant has been rated in these ways, the area admission officer substantiates the numerical evaluation by summarizing the candidate's credentials in a written précis. If the applicant falls at one of the extremes—easily admissable or easily deniable—then the area officer will make that recommendation, and the file will be reviewed by either the director or associate director for a final decision. The remaining files will be reviewed by a second reader, usually another admission officer or a member of the faculty or administration, who will follow the same procedure. This process results in three groups of students: those the college clearly wants to admit, those unqualified for admission, and those who compose the large gray middle of our or any applicant pool—solid candidates, perfectly capable of good academic citizenship.

How then is the rest of the class chosen? By committee, of course, though the vision of a secret inner sanctum is not nearly as glamorous in reality as it seems. (Our own committee room is not wood paneled; it is a rather plain place, more cell-like than club-like, an image that should bring you some solace if you're feeling sorry for yourself in mid-March.) Admission committees, though their components vary from college to college, all have the same function—to make the difficult choices. Files brought to committee are presented by the area officers, who serve as advocates or not, depending on their own review. Candidates are presented, recommendations are given, discussion and argument ensue, and decisions are finally made. All of the candidates can do the work. What seems to matter most at this juncture, what seems to make some applicants come alive or stand apart from the large gray mass, is the committee's sense that they will contribute to the life of the community. Some, for sheer quality of mind and intellectual ability, will be the stars of the classroom, and some will be the campus leaders, the musicians in the orchestra, the writers on the newspaper. Others, for reasons of background, or upbringing, or circumstances of birth, will lend a different perspective or outlook. Still others—those who are just "good folks"—will make fine roommates, enliven a dormitory, or help out whenever needed. All of these people will contribute to the community and benefit from one another's company.

Sound easy? Not when you have lots of kids who can fit the bill. Long hours and a good bit of hard work and soul searching go into the selection process. We like to think the decisions we make are fair, at least as we see them, which implies something else about the process that anyone applying to college should know. The decisions are subjective. Though based in part on objective criteria (grades, scores, letters), they are finally personal judgments of a number of different factors. This subjectivity is what accounts for equally competitive colleges making different decisions on the same applicant. Different people are doing the judging.

So my advice to anyone entering into this careful yet subjective college selection process is to avoid the all-too-common mistake of tying all your hopes to one college or one group of colleges, of creating the perfect mythic place. That place usually doesn't exist and, in fact, most people can be perfectly happy at any number of colleges. The trick to this matter of college application is to investigate and then apply to a group of schools varying in degree of selectivity— some of which are highly competitive, others of which are less so, but all of which can satisfy you academically, extracurricularly, socially, and geographically. The happiest high school senior come April is the one who can look at his or her college list and say, "You know, it almost doesn't matter where I get in. Because wherever I go, I will be happy, satisfied, and prepared to be successful."

75

This attitude, this perspective if you will, is one that everyone applying to college should strive for.

Columbia University is a four-year private liberal arts college for men and women, located in New York, New York.

Applications Admission Counselors Love to Hate

Colleges package themselves. And so do students. Although the large majority of applications are careful, sincere, and honest packages, there are a few every year that are sure to make admission counselors groan:

- ❏ **The "nouvelle" application.** Flashy and glitzy, this application presents the student like a new ice-cream bar; it includes several professional-quality photos and a life résumé hot off the press of some high-tech, high-gloss printing house. Like the stylish cuisine of the seventies, things here look terrific, even artful, but one comes away still hungry for something substantial.
- ❏ **The "new wave" application.** Advised to be different, this applicant has ended up being eccentric. The application arrives inside a coconut shell or hand-lettered in neo-Gothic on a parchment scroll. (Admission counselors can't read neo-Gothic!) The essay is about the student's Victorian tortoise-shell button collection, and the activities list includes varsity football, poet-in-residence, and tour guide for the class trip to Nepal. Appended is a list of patents applied for and a video

tape of the new rap version of *Hamlet* that the applicant lists as a "work in progress."

☐ **The "heavy" application.** This applicant has mustered the forces of the universe on her or his behalf. There are support letters from several different teachers, alumni, employers, chance acquaintances, and irrelevant others. All lists—activities, awards, jobs, interests—exceed the space provided, and several portfolios have been sent under separate cover. This applicant seems to be asking for more than a fair share of the evaluator's time and may be trying to bury a poor academic performance under a heap of assertions that the applicant is "just right" for old Alma Mater U.

☐ **The "light" application.** This applicant hardly had time to apply. He or she may even have used one school's application to apply to another, just crossing out the name of the first institution and penciling in the name of the second. (After all, it's "almost the same stuff.") There are numerous misspellings, omissions, and incomplete sections. The essays are each five sentences long. The tone is flippant, bored, or rushed. Colleges take their admission process seriously and hope their applicants will, too.

BOSTON UNIVERSITY

> "We'd love to eavesdrop on a college admission committee. How will they discuss our child's application folder?"

Daniel Murray
Director of Admission

"I know he's a good student. They're all good students. But they don't all want to go into medicine for the money. He does and I don't like that. There was no humanity in his application at all. At best I'd wait-list him."

"Right. He's so different from the last student. The last one was really alive. There was no arrogance about him. He enjoys life and it shows. He really cares about people. This student is so competitive, so single-minded, so serious about everything, I don't think he belongs in our program."

"But look at those test scores. He has 1430 on his SATs and he broke 700 on every Achievement Test but English. Even if you don't want to admit him—and I think we should—you at least have to give him a place on the wait list."

The discussion goes on for another ten minutes. The great test scores aren't enough. Neither is the 3.9 grade point average. The student is put on the wait list. Others with lower scores are admitted. Others with lower grades are admitted.

You are sitting with the selection committee for Boston University's accelerated program in liberal arts and medicine. This is no ordinary college admission committee. Its staff is trying to decide which high school seniors will make the best physicians. The class they select will enter the university as freshmen in the College of Liberal Arts. Then, after three years, these students will move across town to take their places as first-year students at the medical school.

The competition for admission into Boston's accelerated program is stiff. Long before the selection committee meets, the admission staff reviews the folders of approximately six hundred applicants. This review eliminates more than two-thirds of the candidates. The students who don't make the "first cut" are considered for admission to other programs at the university, and most are admitted.

The committee meeting continues. Sitting at the table are a representative from the admission office and faculty members from both the Medical School and the College of Liberal Arts. The next candidate is from Texas. We'll call him Hari. He has been interviewed by three people: an English professor, a biology professor, and the assistant director of admission. Written summaries of each interview are in the student's folder.

The interviewers disagree about how strong a candidate Hari is. All of them note his excitement when he speaks of medical research—discovering cures, developing cheaper and safer treatments for diseases. The biology professor thinks Hari lacks "a real understanding for the human side of medicine." The English professor, however, has asked the student why he is more interested in research than in treatment. Hari has spoken of a trip his family took to visit relatives in India. He has talked about the disease and poverty he saw and has become almost angry when describing the dirty water people draw from the wells and the poorly trained "nurses" who visit his grandmother's village once a week.

"That sure sounds like the human side of medicine to me," says one of the committee members.

Hari is still in the running.

"Let's look at his junior year record," another committee member says.

The committee turns to the admission officer, who rattles off the courses and grades for Hari's junior year: English, B; precalculus, A; chemistry, A; physics, B +; history, B.

"Good, but not great," says a med school professor.

"They were all honors courses," replies the admission officer.

"All of these kids took honors courses," says the med school prof, "and most of them earned straight A's. As I said, 'Good, but not great.'"

Hari's chances are weakening.

"What about his test scores?" someone asks.

The SAT scores total 1290, but the verbal score is only 580. The Achievement Test scores show the same pattern: math, 740; chemistry, 720; English, 590; American history, 600.

Next, a quick look at Hari's list of activities: science club, math club, junior engineering society. The activities show depth but no breadth at all because everything involves science or math.

Then one of the committee members reviews the recommendations: personal initiative, emotional maturity, and energy all "truly outstanding" (top 2 to 3 percent); motivation, creativity, leadership, self-discipline, and seven other factors all "excellent" (top 10 percent but not top 2 to 3 percent). The committee member votes no.

Someone notes that although Hari was born and raised in this country, his parents were not. Could that have had an effect on his verbal test score? And what about his part-time job? He has worked between ten and twenty hours a week to save money for college. Shouldn't the committee consider that when they look at his school activities? The committee agrees. They think Hari's chances of success in the program are good, but they are not ready to admit him. They place his name on the waiting list. If other, better students turn down an offer of admission, Hari will be allowed to take one of their places.

The committee turns to the next folder. "Stan" is from Long Island. One of his interviewers writes that Stan is "very fast and very loud" when he speaks. "He speaks well, but he doesn't listen." Another interviewer writes, "Stan is sure of himself. He gets good grades, scores well on tests, and plays three varsity sports." Sports are important to Stan. In one interview he has said, "The inner rush of competition is addictive." In another he has said that football is his favorite sport because of the "high visibility" that football players have in the eyes of other students.

Stan is bright. He has earned A's in all his courses, and his SAT scores are 720 verbal and 740 math. He has scored between 690 and 740 on several Achievement Tests, with a 620 in Spanish after only two years of study. During his freshman year in high school he has taken three honors courses, and in his junior year he has earned A's in three advanced placement courses: biology, literature, and calculus.

One of Stan's teachers writes that "Stan has a capacity for work that is intimidating." Another writes that Stan "is an unusually bright young man with extraordinary academic talent." There is no question about Stan's academic ability, and the committee spends little time discussing that. Instead, the committee members want to know what kind of person Stan is. What kind of a doctor will he be? Are his interests any broader than Hari's? Stan has listed six activities on his application. One is the science club, and the other five are athletic pursuits.

"What does he say about himself?" someone asks. "Let's look at his essays."

The committee members shuffle through their papers to find their notes on his essays. There is no time to read a full essay at the meeting. All the reading has been done beforehand. The essays are well written. Stan writes of discovering science through his early interest in space exploration. He also writes about the first "real" science course he took in seventh grade. He makes science sound interesting, challenging, exciting. Most of the committee members are impressed by the essays.

But someone from the med school asks, "Did any of you pick up on those comments about the chemistry class? Talk about arrogance."

The essay is pulled from the folder. Page two, paragraph two: "Then I took chemistry and it was a disaster. I was no longer in an honors class, where everybody knew what they were doing, but rather with all types of students some of whom did not know their left from their right. I therefore lacked interest in the class and in the material itself."

Papers then are pushed aside and the committee talks about Stan. He's a very good student, maybe a great student, but his interviews and essays reveal a person whom several committee members don't like very much. Someone suggests that Stan should be forced to write an essay on humility or compassion. Two people keep talking about grades, test scores, and talent.

Finally, the chairman looks at his watch and calls for a decision. Stan is a much better student than Hari—better courses, better grades, better scores—but the committee doesn't think the personal qualities measure up. Great students don't always make good doctors. Stan is denied admission to the accelerated program but is offered a place in the regular premed program. His supporters on the committee offer the hope that he will mature during his four years as an undergraduate.

The next candidate, a young woman from Kentucky, is "brilliant, concerned, and curious" according to a letter from her school principal. "Marie" is in the math club and the science club, as Hari and Stan are, but she is also an editor of her school paper, an officer in the drama club, and a board member of a citywide youth group. She sings in the school chorus, plays in the school orchestra, and tutors two sixth graders in math. During the summers she spends between twenty and thirty hours each week as a hospital volunteer. She has volunteered in a cancer ward one summer, in a physical therapy department during another. Under "activities" on her application for admission she writes, "See Attachment A." Attachment A is two pages long. Marie does everything and she seems to do it all very well.

One of her essays deals with something she doesn't do well. Marie is not a star athlete like Stan is. She's not even a very good athlete. She writes about trying out for the basketball team and not making it. She writes about trying out again. And again. Finally, she writes about the first basket she ever made in a varsity game. "It wasn't a game-winning basket. It was just a push shot from a foul line, but when it swished through, I froze in disbelief."

The "numbers": 4.0 grade point average, seven advanced placement courses, four honors courses, SAT scores of 740 verbal and 720 math, all Achievement Test scores over 700, and Advanced Placement Examination scores of 5 (the highest possible) in biology, French, and European history.

According to her interviewers, Marie is as impressive in person as she is on paper. She tells of being three or four years old and wanting to "grow up, change into a boy, and become a doctor." Then she talks about how exciting it is for her to realize that today some of the best doctors she knows are women.

Marie is admitted to our accelerated program. There aren't many Maries in the world, but there are enough of them so that even a good student like Hari or a very good student like Stan finds the competition for admission to a program like this one very stiff indeed.

Boston University is a four-year private university for men and women, located in Boston, Massachusetts.

OBERLIN COLLEGE

> "We know college admission directors
> are only human, but how much do
> their personalities influence how they
> choose candidates?"

J. Leon Washington
Director of Admission

An admission staff is a motley crew exhibiting, perhaps, the widest range of diversity of experiences and backgrounds that can be found on a college campus. Members of this crew share a love of learning, an enthusiastic spirit, an eclectic style, a keen sense of detail, an ability to think fast on their feet, and of course, the gift of gab! They are often generalists, yet they harbor deep underlying commitments to causes they will defend at all costs. And so it happens they often have very strong opinions and sometimes are even stubborn. They are articulate and they are very good listeners. But above all, they are individuals with distinct personalities.

The personalities of a college's admission staff have a direct influence on the composition of every freshman class admitted to the institution. A stellar, well-informed, enthusiastic staff usually results in a stellar, well-informed, enthusiastic group of students. Generally speaking, the wider the range of personalities on the admission staff, the more multitalented the candidates admitted. As Jim Montoya, director of admission at Vassar College in Poughkeepsie, New York, says, "If in fact we wish to seek a diverse student body, it seems to me that it is my responsibility as the director to maintain a diverse admission staff. It is human nature to be attracted to individuals who possess those qualities we most approve of in ourselves."

The personalities of the admission staff members can also determine, for the most part, the so-called "fit" or adaptability of candidates to a particular campus. As staff members, they have settled into the campus, and they have absorbed aspects of the campus environment into their personalities. As a result, they can often tell with relative ease which candidates will have trouble fitting into the environment and which candidates will not.

During a recent selection committee meeting of our admission staff at Oberlin, we took a look at some personality traits exhibited by staff members to see what impact those traits had on decisions we were making. Although our survey was not a scientific experiment complete with empirical data, we found that every member of the staff had his or her "favorite" student types, his or her peculiar likes and dislikes. For example:

- ☐ Staff members with strict, "serious" personalities rated tougher on academics than did those who might be labeled "less serious."
- ☐ Members of the staff who were very involved in their careers in admission looked for similar involvement on the part of the candidates in their high schools.
- ☐ Staff members who were athletically inclined were more apt to support candidates with strong athletic ability but only average academic ability than were those staff members who were not athletically inclined.
- ☐ Minorities and women on the staff were more sensitive to issues surrounding the selection of minority candidates than were nonminority males.
- ☐ Men on the staff were generally more supportive of male candidates, and women on the staff were generally more supportive of female candidates.
- ☐ Every staff member had his or her peculiar tastes for a particular style of writing, and some even had a preference for the strange or unusual writing sample.

❑ Some staff members were attracted to candidates from certain parts of the country; all were attracted to candidates from their own hometowns or high schools.

In general, we found that the members of our admission staff were readily drawn to the defense of candidates with whom they had things in common—and the more they had in common, the stronger the attraction.

The goal of every college selection process is to amass a group of students who are well qualified, well rounded, intelligent, competent, flexible, interesting, and possessed of a good sense of humor. It appears that the only way to achieve this end is to have an admission staff with a mix of personalities that will set the selection wheel in motion. Because personality is such an important factor, admission offices—large and small, public and private—usually are composed of a broad array of personalities—men and women, young and old, novices and well-seasoned troopers—in hopes that such a configuration will bring to the college students who can readily blend into the campus and still retain a sense of who they are. It seems to me that since college admission involves making judgments about the intelligence, ability, and character of individuals, useful yardsticks of measurement in the process are the personalities, knowledge, and experience of those who are judging.

Oberlin College is a four-year private college of arts and sciences for men and women, located in Oberlin, Ohio.

HARVARD AND RADCLIFFE COLLEGES

"How can our child get into Harvard?"

David L. Evans
Senior Admission Officer

Like many of our colleagues, we in the Harvard and Radcliffe Admission Office must annually choose a class from an applicant pool many times larger than the number we enroll. That some 80 to 90 percent of the candidates wishing to come to Cambridge are academically qualified to do Harvard work presents a considerable challenge for us in making our final decisions.

We are fortunate to have six times as many *qualified* applicants as we can admit. But fortune, like roses, is usually accompanied by thorns. The "thorns" with which we must deal come not from admitting the one applicant deemed most qualified, but from the frustration in turning away the other five who could also have successful careers at Harvard. Frankly, there is no easy way to deny admission to such talented young men and women.

Some might say that the sheer size of such a talented applicant pool makes any method short of random selection difficult to explain. We disagree. A "luck-of-the-draw" approach assumes that all candidates with the requisite academic credentials are somehow *equally* qualified and that no other issues are considered in the admission process. Obviously, there are academic differences even among the most gifted candidates, and, furthermore, our campuses would be much less interesting if academic talent were our *only* criterion.

These varying degrees of qualification permit us to establish a hierarchy among the qualified applicants. The class is then chosen from this group of very strong candidates. The easiest to admit are those whose objective credentials, rigorous course work, and informed recommendations suggest that they are potential scholars of the first order. In the Harvard and Radcliffe Admission Office, this number usually varies between two hundred and four hundred out of approximately fourteen thousand applicants. This is less than 10 to 20 percent of the twenty-one hundred students admitted annually. Consequently, the bulk of our yearly task is selecting the remaining eighteen hundred or so from about twelve thousand qualified candidates.

The selection process is exhaustive and, to use a term from economics, labor intensive, but it is manageable. We have our predecessors in admission to thank for solving most of the problems normally encountered in a bureaucracy of this size. We are, therefore, able to read the application folders as many as four times.

Although eminently significant to the candidates and to Harvard, selection is not the totality of the admission process. Recruitment, which precedes folder reading and admission selection meetings, is equally comprehensive and involves literally thousands of Harvard and Radcliffe representatives. During a typical school year about twenty thousand prospective applicants are contacted by one or more of the following groups with official ties to the admission office: the admission staff, the alumni Schools and Scholarships Committee, and undergraduate student volunteers.

The Schools and Scholarships Committee is by far the largest of the three groups, and its members are located in all fifty states and many foreign countries. These very enthusiastic graduates of the university visit schools and college-day programs, award prizes (usually books) to outstanding juniors, raise scholarship funds, and interview applicants to Harvard and Radcliffe Colleges. Much of the success of our admission and financial aid offices results from the efforts of these men and women.

Second in size to the Schools and Scholarships Committee are the undergraduate student volunteers. These sophomores, juniors, and seniors are trained by the admission office to travel as official representatives for us. All of their travel is coordinated with the admission staff member responsible for the area they will visit. Additionally, a formal letter of introduction is sent to the high schools to be visited, and the local Schools and Scholarships Committee is also notified of their coming. Not only do these undergrads enable us to visit many more high schools than we could ordinarily, but their ages often give them more "credibility" with prospective applicants. Scores of our currently enrolled students attribute their attendance here to the convincing presentation made by a "student rep."

Last, but not least, are the thirty-five admission staff members with specific geographic and school responsibilities. Each of us visits our areas and schools annually. While traveling, we talk to interested students, guidance counselors, parents, and others about opportunities in Cambridge. A great deal of our time, however, is spent dispelling myths about Harvard and Radcliffe. One such myth is that only the rich attend Harvard; the truth is that approximately 70 percent of the undergraduates receive some form of financial aid. Another myth with slightly less currency maintains that "only students with the highest grades and SAT scores need apply to Harvard." This fable is probably rooted in the fact that the *median* grade point average and SAT scores of the classes admitted to Harvard each year are among the highest in the country. It ignores the *range* of those grades and scores, however. For example, SAT scores of admitted students extend from a low of approximately 1,050 to a high of 1,600. Grades, too, usually vary from a solid B + average to perfection. But I cannot remember any admitted student whose grades *and* scores were at the lower end of both spectra. As a rule, if an academic risk is taken, it is taken on candidates whose grades are exceptionally high but whose SAT scores might be more modest.

Our quest for an intellectually, socially, economically, geographically, culturally, extracurricularly, and personally diverse student body annually takes us to all the states of the United States, several territories, and Canada. Occasionally, one or two staff members also go to Europe and beyond. This recruitment is costly and time-consuming, but the dynamic mix of students resulting from it makes it well worthwhile.

Once the applications have been submitted, the three hundred or so academic superstars admitted, and the approximately two thousand unqualified candidates rejected, the long and tedious selection process begins.

Applications are graded in essentially three categories: academics, personal qualities or character, and extracurricular activities. Besides academics—the range of grades and SAT scores necessary to place a candidate "in the ballpark"—the other two categories are also important for admission.

We view our task of assembling a class with a "split vision"; that is, we must choose the "best" individual and that individual must, at the same time, fit into the "best" class. In so doing, we look for personal qualities that promote individual as well as group development, respect, awareness of community issues (local, national, and global), compassion, intellectual verve, and scholarly inquisitiveness. We also look for those movers and shakers with a sense of consequence, whether it is as a school or community leader or as a quiet force for good in daily life.

We learn about students' personal characteristics from several sources. The two required teachers' reports tell us a great deal. Much is also revealed in the secondary school report that is usually submitted by the guidance counselor. Additionally, there is ample opportunity for the student to make his or her own case in the application. The application form provides enough room to list work experiences, extracurricular activities, and honors, as well as additional space. Brief statements about academic and nonacademic college goals are required, and the two-hundred-to-five-hundred-word essay can cover *any* topic the candidate wants to address.

Because nearly all of our applicants have interviews in the cities or towns where they attend school, we also have the benefit of personal interaction between students and alumni when we try to assess character.

Although personal qualities is probably the most subjective category of the application, it isn't taken lightly. We go to great lengths to learn something about the human being behind the grades and scores. When all of the school reporting, student essays, and alumni interview reports are totaled, it is not unusual to have fifteen hundred words in an application folder that help us appraise the personal qualities of the candidate.

The final category in which we judge our applicants is extracurricular activities. We look for energy, leadership, and creativity wherever it is found, whether it is in student government, music, field hockey, religious youth groups, drama, Boy Scouts, football, or any of hundreds of other nonacademic endeavors. If a student has to commute great distances, work long hours, or is disabled and thereby prevented from involvement in nonacademic activities, this expectation is waived.

It is with this process of recruiting large numbers of talented students from all quarters of our society and world, of assessing their folders with an eye toward a diverse and dynamic student body, and then bringing them to Cambridge that we sustain the "magic" of this job and the wonder of the undergraduates who pass through the Harvard and Radcliffe portals.

Harvard and Radcliffe Colleges is a four-year private liberal arts college for men and women, located in Cambridge, Massachusetts.

Testing: The Hard Numbers

"The toad, without which no garden would be complete."

—CHARLES DUDLEY WARNER

Select the sentence below that most correctly describes the role of standardized college entrance tests:

(A) Standardized test scores are the most important bit of information in a candidate's application folder.

(B) All colleges require college entrance tests for admission.

(C) Coaching and review courses are guaranteed ways to increase test scores.

(D) Fabulous test scores can make up for a poor or incomplete high school record.

(E) None of the above.

Unless you said, "None of the above," you have something to learn about your child's testing and scores. About all that's certain is that you're no doubt extremely grateful you don't have to take them now yourself. Whether your teen is planning to take the SAT (Scholastic Aptitude Test) or the ACT (American College Testing Program Assessment), he or she is going to feel a great deal of understandable and perhaps even some not-so-understandable anxiety before test day. Moreover, he or she is going to have to sort out a lot of myth, information, and conflicting research to fully understand the results after test day.

Some students let the difficulty of taking college entrance tests grow into mountainous proportions. One student, for instance, devoted her entire senior year to the college admission process, most of it to preparing for the SAT. Between the SAT prep course her high school offered during her study hall period, another SAT prep course offered by a local coaching company during the evenings, and an application-essay writing course given by her senior English teacher, her course work and extracurricular activities really suffered. She actually spent her chemistry lectures flipping through SAT vocabulary flashcards! Before you let your child get carried away, as this student did, with "preparation tactics," think about the choices to the opening question:

Choice (A) is false because test scores are *not* the most important information college admission people consider when reviewing your child's application folder. Several admission directors throughout the book make this point loud and clear. It is the high school program and academic record that carry the most weight.

Choice (B) is false because not all schools require the same thing in the way of tests. A few institutions recently have decided on ethical grounds to make SAT and ACT test scores optional for admission. Bates College is one of those institutions, and its dean of admission explains why.

Choice (C) is obviously false because review courses can't *guarantee* raising scores on tests, and you and your child should be wary of laying out cash for courses that promise they can. Because college admission directors have only secondhand knowledge of coaching courses, the rage of the eighties, we went straight to a high school guidance counselor and asked her how students were faring on college entrance exams after intensive preparation.

Choice (D) is false because the exact opposite is true. It's the fabulous high school record that can outweigh average or even poor test scores. Read Jim Rogers from Brown University on the importance of the high school record.

93

You can help your teen take tests in stride by devising a game plan:

- ❑ Decide together that your teen will take the SAT or ACT once, late in the junior year. Then, if scores seem low, he or she can take the test one more time. Bear in mind, though, that repeated testing rarely leads to magnificent results. One student, for instance, took the SAT five times, and each time a 50-point increase in one section was offset by a 50-point decrease in the other. The investment of time and money didn't pay off.
- ❑ Help your child prepare for the SAT or ACT without coaching first. The College Board and the American College Testing Program provide materials to prepare for their tests. Getting used to the format and the types of questions is half the battle (and a lot of what prep courses do for students). Your child should *not* try to memorize long lists of obscure words; it is much more realistic to prepare for the math sections of these tests than to try to learn the dictionary by November 7.
- ❑ If you and your child choose a test preparation course, make sure you shop around for a reputable company that teaches relevant test-taking skills and uses *real* practice tests. Watch out for the "beat-the-test" mentality. It sounds great but it's no substitute for knowledge.

Besides taking a couple of entrance tests, your teen has a year or more of high school to live through—basic courses, honors courses, band or football or drama practice, proms—and that time is supposed to be educational and enjoyable. Senior year is what freshmen dream about. Help your son or daughter concentrate on learning, enjoying, and keeping the tests in perspective. Remember, after your teen is accepted into a college, no one will ever ask or care about what his or her tests scores were again!

INDEPENDENT COLLEGE COUNSELOR

> ## "How do admission committees view SAT scores? Are they a deciding factor in selecting applicants?"

James W. Wickenden, Jr.
Wickenden Associates, Princeton, New Jersey
Former Dean of Admission at Princeton University

While believing that standardized tests can make a constructive and positive contribution to the admission process, I also believe that some of the recent criticism of the tests is justified. Several issues relating to the use of test scores in the admission process deserve mention.

In the first place, I have serious reservations about those colleges and universities that tie admission to only two variables—grade point average and SAT scores. Not only does such a policy ignore critically important information about the personal characteristics and non-academic talents of the applicants, but also it assumes a degree of accuracy in predicting academic success that the SAT has not demonstrated. While a correlation indeed does exist between test performance and grades in the first year of college, the relationship is far from perfect. For example, a few years ago, Princeton accepted a young woman with a verbal score of 300, some 350 points below the mean score for other accepted applicants. Because she was the valedictorian of her high school class and had been in this country only five years, Princeton decided to disregard her SAT performance. At the end of her first year there, she had three A's, three B's, and two C's. Yet a college with an SAT "floor" might not have accepted her.

Second, the SAT places a premium on speed. Therefore, students who are careful, thoughtful, and considered in their judgments may be penalized as they wrestle with the subtleties of complex questions.

Third, I am concerned about the effects the tests can have on the self-esteem of those who take them. Students who score at the national mean on the verbal portion of the SAT may think of themselves as "only a 430," and they may question their intellectual abilities. What needs to be emphasized is that the SAT is not intended to measure adaptability, motivation, creativity, native talent, or the capacity to succeed in a particular occupation. Instead, it is designed simply to measure *developed ability*. This measurement is used by admission officers to make a reasoned prediction of a student's academic performance in the first year of college, but it must be used with sensitivity and with an understanding of the applicant's background.

Finally, I am concerned that many who work in admission and spend a good portion of the year interpreting test scores may have little or no training in tests and measurements.

Despite these concerns, I nevertheless advocate responsible use of standardized tests in the admission process.

Although critics of the Educational Testing Service (ETS) claim otherwise, I firmly believe that the services provided by that organization have helped talented minority-group and disadvantaged applicants gain admission to selective colleges. Those black, Hispanic, and native American applicants who participate in the minority-search program offered by ETS and who perform well on the SAT receive literally hundreds of letters from colleges across the country seeking them as applicants. I am persuaded that the SAT has opened more doors than it has closed for minority-group and disadvantaged students.

If the SAT were abolished, admission officers would have no alternative other than to rely on grades, rank in class, and evaluations by teachers and counselors. These vary tremendously in quality from school to school.

Without the SAT, some institutions might revert to earlier practices and develop their own admission tests. In all likelihood such tests would be inferior to those developed by ETS. Moreover, they would vary substantially in quality and content from institution to institution, and they would require students interested in several institutions either to take a range of tests (if schedules could be worked out) or to limit the number of schools to which they could apply.

Given the above, what would I recommend?

First, colleges and universities that tie admission decisions to an arbitrarily determined level of performance on the SAT should reconsider that policy.

Second, colleges and universities with flexible admission policies should ensure that the admission officers interpreting these scores are adequately trained in tests and measurements. Moreover, those colleges should conduct annual studies to determine which of the variables in the admission process are the best predictors of academic success at their institutions.

Third, ETS should continue to improve and refine its procedures, free from the kind of legislative interference that might make the SAT less valid, more expensive, or less frequently offered.

The SAT, like any other standardized test, is an imperfect instrument. Despite its imperfections, it is a useful piece in the admission puzzle.

James W. Wickenden heads Wickenden Associates, an educational counseling and consulting service in Princeton, New Jersey, that helps parents and their teenagers with the admission process to colleges and independent secondary schools.

BROWN UNIVERSITY

"Our child has marvelous college entrance test scores but a shaky high school record. What will this mean for acceptance?"

James H. Rogers
Director of Admission

When I entered admission work in 1965, I did not anticipate how comforting it would be for me to know in advance what kinds of pressures I would face at any given time during the academic year. The joy one feels in addressing an eager young audience in the fall is balanced by the pain of sending out many denial letters in the spring. There are a thousand encounters that repeat themselves each year, over and over again, and one gets pretty good at handling the issues and questions, especially those involving college entrance test scores and high school records.

For instance, sometime between May and September, usually during our commencement, I can expect a phone call that goes something like this: "Well, Jim, I won't be bothering you with our son Jason's application. We've talked it over and realize that, although his SAT scores are very good, his grades are below what I know Brown wants." As I hang up the phone, I know that I will have a future conversation with Jason's father. Most likely a second telephone call will come in December, after the family has had a chance to review Jason's college options during the Thanksgiving holidays.

Two things will have occurred since I last talked with Jason's father. Both are predictable; they repeat themselves with frequency at this time in the admission cycle. First, the parents come face-to-face with the hard reality that Jason cannot possibly be admitted to Brown unless he applies to Brown. Second, they see a miracle in the making: Jason's grades have improved tremendously. "Dammit, Doris, he can make it at Brown. I'm going to give Jim Rogers a ring."

The first mistake Jason's parents are making is that they are not considering their son's true educational needs. They are looking for what *they* perceive to be best for Jason without considering Jason at all. What they are doing is putting Jason into competition he cannot meet and setting him up for what they will perceive as failure—all because of the social cachet associated with a son or daughter going to a college whose name is recognized throughout the United States, at least by the friends they want to impress. In a sense, the parents' child-rearing practices are on the line at college admission time, and they do not want to admit to anything less than perfection.

But wait, Jason's grades are better. Maybe he *is* a good match for Brown. Before I receive the phone call from the father or open Jason's application for review, I know what I will find. Whether Jason has had difficulty with math, science, foreign language, or social sciences, he will have found a way to drop most of those courses with which he has struggled in the past. I would like to find that in place of French IV he has substituted advanced placement American history or advanced placement calculus, but this will not be the case. Jason will have taken the minimum number of courses required and the easiest electives available to a senior. His course selection might well look something like this:

- ❑ English IV
- ❑ Film & Society
- ❑ Sociology
- ❑ Choir
- ❑ Photography

There is nothing wrong with a senior-year course load like this, depending upon Jason's objectives and interests. For Brown, such a

99

curriculum is inappropriate. As an academically rigorous undergraduate institution, Brown expects successful applicants to have stretched themselves in the classroom and to have taken the most difficult academic program available to them in their high school.

There may be many reasons why a student does not select all of the most difficult courses in his or her school, but most academically demanding undergraduate colleges want their students to have taken the following:

- ❑ Four years of English, with a heavy emphasis on writing
- ❑ Four years of mathematics, continued through the senior year
- ❑ Three years of laboratory sciences
- ❑ Four years of a foreign language, continued through the senior year
- ❑ Three years of social sciences, including American history
- ❑ Electives in art, music, and computer science

Most students do not have all of these courses when they enter college, but it is clear from their course selection that they have taken the most challenging ones available to them and have not avoided major academic areas for lack of interest or ability.

Jason is a typical bright young man, as reflected in his strong SAT scores, but he has not chosen to challenge himself and as such is not a strong candidate for a highly selective institution. His interests are most likely in nonacademic areas. There's nothing wrong with that. Some of the most successful people in later life are those who had considerable difficulty in high school. Where one goes to college has little to do with success in later life. Motivation, perseverance, drive, originality, and creativity have a great deal to do with how well one does in the world after college. Although these elements are important in college selection, the simple fact remains that the best indicator of academic success in college is academic success in high school. A high-testing, low-achieving student is a student who, for some reason, cannot harness his or her abilities to be successful academically.

Each year I hear a lot more about low-testing, high-achieving candidates than I do about Jason and others like him. Here the lament goes something like this: "I don't understand it. Jane ranks academically near the top of her class, is editor-in-chief of the yearbook, plays the flute in the band, is regionally ranked in tennis, gets rave reviews from teachers, and yet her SAT scores are terrible. There's something wrong with the system when our daughter can have her chances at a good college ruined by a three-hour test."

Jane's case is much more common than Jason's. From May through March we hear about poor testers. Probably there are as many reasons for poor performance on the standardized tests used in college admission as there are students who fall into this category. Although everyone reacts differently to testing, there are some valid generalizations that can be made.

First, as I said before, academic achievement in rigorous courses is what counts in selective admission. Poor testing will not help a student's admission, but it should not preclude it.

Second, many students test poorly because they have been poorly educated. If Jane's test scores are at or above the median for her senior class, then she's probably not a poor tester. She simply has not been well prepared for the tests or for a demanding college curriculum. Such candidates often have trouble being admitted to selective institutions. At Brown, we value high-achieving students, but those who have not been well prepared for our rigorous curriculum are not given a spot in our freshmen class because they are forced out by many others who have been well prepared and who have test results that are as good as, or better than, theirs.

Third, "type A" personalities are often not good testers. They have learned over time, as Jane may have, that in order to get something done they must do it personally and they must do it perfectly. These students work extremely hard and are always busy with their homework or some other significant project. Yet this same high motivation and perseverance penalizes them in a timed-test situation. They want to get things right and often spend too much time on questions they don't understand. Consequently, they don't answer enough questions to achieve a high test score. Furthermore, they do not like to guess and be wrong. They get frustrated when they narrow down the answer to one or two options and cannot figure out which is correct. They should guess and move on quickly, but it is against their nature to do so.

Low-testing, high-ranking students are a much better academic risk than high-testing, low-ranking students. We know that Jane would succeed at Brown much better than would Jason. Jason should take time off between high school and college and try to determine what he really wants to do and why he wants to do it. Jane would probably enjoy her four years at Brown and be a more positive force in our student community than Jason would. Jane would also be in social and academic overdrive during her four years at Brown. Some might argue that she would be so busy she would never truly reflect on what she was doing, its purpose and meaning. *Intellectual* is not an adjective that most would apply to Jane, yet it denotes a quality our faculty value greatly.

Most experienced college admission officers can review an applicant's transcript and predict the student's test scores, whether SAT or ACT. The tests designed to be used in college selection are good confirming tools. They tell us what we think we already know from the student's transcript and academic references. For that small group of individuals who have had a good elementary and middle school foundation, who may have read widely and yet do not achieve well (the Jasons of this world), I would recommend that they defer entrance to college and try to determine what they are truly interested in and why. Until something turns them on, they will wander aimlessly through academe. For those like Jane—and there are many more—I say keep up the good work, but slow down a bit to find out why you are working so hard. What is the meaning behind what you are doing? You will be successful, but you should try to determine why you do things the way you do them and, in this way, gain some direction in your life.

Annually, at Brown, we must send denial letters to ten thousand fine young people. As I sign these letters, I read over and over the last line just above my signature. Its truth is little understood by those who receive it, but the message is something all students should take with them as they head off to freshman orientation week: "Remember, in the long run it does not matter so much where you go to college as it does what you go for and with."

Brown University is a four-year private liberal arts university for men and women, located in Providence, Rhode Island.

Brown's Rank in Class and SAT Score Spread for 1987

Here is an example of one highly selective institution's SAT score distribution and rank-in-class figures for 1987. This information can help you compare your child's test scores and ranking with those of other students who were accepted by the institution. Don't read these figures as promises or prohibitions. In the context of the entire application, each child's record tells a different story about his or her high school experience.

RANK IN CLASS

	Applied	Accepted	Percent Accepted	Enrolled
Valedictorian	943	462	48.9%	155
Salutatorian	546	224	41.0%	95
Ranked Third	493	186	37.7%	80
Ranked Fourth	418	150	35.9%	85
Ranked Fifth	403	113	28.0%	56
Subtotal	2,803	1,135	40.5%	471
Other Top Five Percent	1,863	455	24.4%	239
Second Five Percent	2,008	433	21.6%	243
Total Top Tenth	6,674	2,023	30.3%	953
2nd Tenth	1,400	228	16.3%	144
3rd Tenth	631	65	10.3%	48
4th Tenth	410	47	11.5%	36
5th Tenth	209	19	9.1%	13
6th Tenth	68	5	7.3%	4
7th Tenth	78	0	0%	0
8th Tenth	37	0	0%	0
9th Tenth	29	0	0%	0
Bottom Tenth	17	0	0%	0
No Rank	2,933	403	13.5%	226
Total	12,486	2,790	22.3%	1,424

DISTRIBUTION OF SAT SCORES

	VERBAL				MATH			
	Applied	Accepted	Percent Accepted	Enrolled	Applied	Accepted	Percent Accepted	Enrolled
750–800	224	127	57%	32	1,376	538	39%	208
700–749	1,358	536	39%	230	2,623	746	28%	349
650–699	2,431	649	27%	323	3,104	687	22%	383
600–649	2,650	616	23%	346	2,092	393	19%	223
550–599	2,236	390	17%	214	1,414	220	16%	138
500–549	1,626	266	16%	165	733	93	13%	72
450–499	747	85	11%	60	328	29	9%	24
400–449	341	32	9%	24	138	6	4%	5
300–399	233	14	6%	11	66	4	6%	4
200–299	34	1	3%	1	7	0	0%	0
No Test Scores	606	74	12%	18	605	74	12%	18
Total	12,486	2,790	22.3%	1,424	12,486	2,790	22.3%	1,424

Reprinted with the kind permission of Brown University's Admission Office.

BATES COLLEGE

"Why did some colleges drop the SAT as a requirement for admission?"

William C. Hiss
Dean of Admission and Financial Aid

Is the SAT a prolific chicken that lays the golden eggs of good college performance? Or are we holding on fiercely to something that makes no sense just because it provides us with a reassuringly statistical self-definition? Perhaps the truth is somewhere in the middle: that standardized testing is neither on the one hand an irreplaceable chicken nor on the other hand a totally chimerical figment of our neurotic need to justify the wild guesses we make.

At Bates, we decided to study the issue closely. Our research showed that less weight was being given to personal qualities in the admission process than our colleagues in the colleges claimed. Ironically, it also showed that personal qualities like energy and initiative, sense of academic success, intellectual tolerance, assertiveness, motivation, and independence all seemed to be of significant importance in the prediction of eventual grade point average (GPA).

Curiously enough, we found relatively little correlation between students' actual GPAs and their sense of academic success. Many students with high GPAs didn't feel particularly successful; others with relatively modest grades had a very high sense of academic success.

105

We also found important variations in both the academic credentials and the personal qualities that seemed to predict success for male and female students. Yet despite these distinct differences, men and women at Bates earned parallel academic records.

After much careful and heartfelt discussion, Bates finally decided not to require the SAT for admission into the college. In this SAT decision, the faculty wanted to offer a clear and public gesture to encourage applications from students they wanted to teach, students in groups sometimes not likely to have the SATs operating on their behalf: minority students, students with two languages, first-generation immigrants, and students from rural and low-income family backgrounds.

The faculty also discussed at considerable length the current mania among students for coaching courses. We have done considerable research on this and honestly cannot tell whether coaching works or not. My personal, private suspicion is that it works in enough cases to fuel the madness, but we have objections to the coaching either way. If it does work, it is simply one more advantage for the rich. If it does not work, the students are wasting their time, their money, and, probably most important, their self-confidence.

We think coaching distracts attention and inhibits growth at precisely the critical watershed moment when kids need to build up a significant head of personal steam for critical thinking, effective writing, and strong analytical skills. Our decision was an attempt to say to young people, "Use your time and your energy to create real forward motion in your life. Read Dostoyevsky, take advanced placement calculus, work in a resettlement house for immigrants, get involved with Amnesty International, lead the field hockey team—do any of these and as many as you can find time for."

Two other issues about coaching we think are important, one predictive and one ethical. We have not found convincing evidence that coaching will raise students' scores. However, we have found a fairly convincing pattern in our research that suggests that coaching, even if it does raise SAT scores, doesn't raise GPAs.

The students we studied who had been coached were lower on almost every single measure we use: SAT scores, Achievement Test scores, high school grade point average or rank in class, academic ratings—everything. And once they came to Bates, they earned GPAs that were 25 percent below the class average as freshmen and 15 percent below the class average as upperclassmen. Not surprisingly, they were also significantly less concerned with college finances or the necessity to hold campus employment.

A final issue of fairness is the one about which I personally feel the strongest. It does not relate to how testing predicts individual performance, and my brother and sister deans seldom talk about it, I am afraid. It is that low or average scores exert sometimes not very subtle pressure on us to deny students who we may think for other reasons can do good work at our institution. As long as SAT scores are a kind of insidious shorthand or code for the health and quality of an institution, then average scores in each freshman class are going to influence how decisions are made. If SAT scores can be volatile barometers of what people believe the quality of an institution is, then they simply become a self-fulfilling institutional prophecy. My hope is that our decision at Bates will allow for a little bit of light and a new perspective on that issue.

I certainly do not want to convey the impression that the discussion on the Bates faculty was unanimous, thunderously left-wing and right-thinking, or even always polite. But we crossed a Rubicon when a medievalist, getting up to move the legislation, said, "Three years ago, I thought optional SATs were a terrible idea. I have come to feel it may be a dramatic and fine chance to strengthen our applicant pool."

We benefitted from wild, blind luck of the most fantastic sort, as well. For almost two years before we made our decision, Harvard had been talking about making the SAT optional if students would take five Achievement Tests. Largely because they did not want to force students to take two sets of Achievements and therefore increase the amount of testing, Harvard eventually decided not to make the SAT optional. But their open and public consideration of that possibility thoroughly plowed up and harrowed our garden in a way I am not sure we could have done for ourselves.

All during this period—and the legislation was on the floor of the faculty for more than six months before the decision was finally approved—I kept thinking that if Harvard went first, we would be the classic gunboat in the wake of a British battleship. As it turned out, although Harvard's research on the overlap between SAT and Achievement Test scores almost exactly paralleled our own, we went ahead and they decided not to. Bates hit the beginning of a nationwide wave of concern about standardized testing, and for better or worse, we have become the test case.

All schools and colleges float upon the waters of their society and are significantly carried by the currents and winds in which they ride. Those who think they are shaping the future of the college primarily by reading the folders and making decisions are, I think, deluded. Their act is perhaps a little more analogous to rearranging the deck chairs on the Titanic. The real key to admission is not so much who can be admitted as who chooses to apply and enroll. In that sense, our original SAT decision has sent out a very broad signal, if it is heard right, that Bates cares about intellectual integrity, hard work, and real achievement.

Bates College is a four-year private liberal arts college for men and women, located in Lewiston, Maine.

A Guidance Counselor's View of SAT Coaching Courses: Do They Pay Off?

Dona Schwab
Interim Acting Assistant Principal
Bronx High School of Science

More than a hundred thousand college-bound students are coached each year before they take the SAT. Some even suffer from what could be called "coaching madness": they get double-prepped by taking both a group coaching course and private tutoring. As a high school assistant principal and guidance counselor, I think parents should fully understand the test prep phenomenon before their child steps into the coaching ring.

Students can choose from two basic kinds of SAT coaching courses. One kind uses the concept of teaching to increase specific math and vocabulary skills and may even offer access to a tape library of study information. The other kind uses the "beat-the-test-makers" concept to teach test-taking skills based on how the test itself is organized. Both incorporate test-taking techniques. Whatever preparation your child chooses, coaching itself has certain advantages and disadvantages.

Three important advantages to coaching:

- ☐ The "practice factor." Preparation encourages familiarity with the SAT so that students know what types of questions to expect and how to pace themselves in the allotted time.
- ☐ The "comfort factor." Preparation can increase the comfort level of students and thus reduce the anxiety they experience during testing.
- ☐ The "skill-building factor." For some students, preparation can reinforce certain skills that are needed for the test, particularly math skills.

Some disadvantages to coaching:

- ☐ Moral dilemma. Students are given the wrong message that cramming or outsmarting the system, rather than *getting smart* by reading and studying, is the way to tackle challenges.
- ☐ Unrealistic expectations. Some students score high on practice tests and then don't score as well on the real thing.
- ☐ Complacency. Like unrealistic expectations, high scores on practice tests can lead to a complacent attitude about the real test.
- ☐ Inequality of opportunity. Although some scholarships are available, not everyone has access to or can afford test preparation.   ▶

There is no organized SAT test prep course at the Bronx High School of Science, although some teachers use SAT-type questions in their classrooms to teach certain English and mathematics concepts. A good many Bronx Science students do take commercial coaching courses or the free New York City Saturday coaching course offered to all high school students at various sites throughout the city (Bronx Science is one site).

Based on my experience with students, I recommend exposure to some form of test preparation to develop test familiarity and increase motivation. Taking a course with other college-bound students can be a stimulant. Meeting others with a drive to succeed often encourages students to perform better. This is especially helpful to students whose peers may not be college bound. But the best preparation for the SAT is long-range basic skill building. Read, read, read! I do think *review* coaching sends a better message to sttudents than beat-the-test-makers coaching. I tell my students, "Long-term skill building pays off. Beating the system may pay off for the moment, but it's not the way to go. If you've already developed the skills needed to succeed in college, your SAT scores should reflect this."

Profiles of the Two Biggest
Commercial Coaching Courses

Stanley H. Kaplan Educational Center	*The Princeton Review*
$450	$565
11-week course, 1 class per week	6-week course, 3 classes per week
Diagnostic test	Diagnostic test
Classes; mock SAT; practice tapes	Classes; mock SAT

Partial scholarships	Scholarships; work-study jobs
Dissatisfied students repeat course free	Dissatisfied students repeat course free
Teaches math and verbal skills useful for SAT and college	Teaches test-taking skills and how test writers think
4 to 6 hours of homework per week	

Six Points to Consider When Picking a Coaching School

1. Does the school teach test-taking skills or basic math and verbal skills or both?
2. Does the school teach skills that are relevant or skills that will never be tested? Who is actually teaching the course? Are home study materials provided?
3. Does the school diagnose students before teaching them?
4. What are the school's class sizes?
5. Are students offered a guarantee to increase test scores by a certain number of points? Can students repeat the course free of charge if not satisfied?
6. Are scholarships available?

The Competitive High School Record

"An Education is ... the compensation of a great deal of thought in the compassing and a great deal of trouble in the attaining."

—JOHN HENRY NEWMAN

If there is anything like agreement in the college admission business, it is that the high school record stands as the primary source of information about a candidate. Poor test scores may not keep your teen out of the school of his or her choice. Neither may a predictable essay with nothing especially wonderful to say. But let's face it, the high school record is a history of four years of sustained effort, a chronicle of decisions, and a reliable and significant source of information about skills, choices, attitudes, and all sorts of things your child needs to have mastered in order to succeed in college. Certainly it's not the whole story. We all like to console ourselves with the fact that Abraham Lincoln didn't finish high school or that Thomas Edison dropped out. But like it or not, there is a strong correlation between success in high school and success in college. Of all the credentials, then, the high school record will receive the most attention by a college admission committee, and it will do the most to help or hurt your child's chances of acceptance.

The high school record *should* be primary in the evaluation of candidates. Standardized test scores are but a snapshot of your child's performance on a single day. Moreover, there is a fair amount of controversy over what these tests really measure—whether they favor men and upper-middle-class test takers, whether review courses are invalidating the results, and whether as a nation we should be evaluating our school systems by the test scores they produce. (The tests were *never* intended to be used as a measure of a curriculum or school system.) The high school record is considered primary in the evaluation of college applicants because, in most cases, it has a significant degree of objectivity and reliability.

Grades are important. Colleges will look at grade point average as well as individual grades in specific subjects. Grades will be considered in light of both the courses your child has taken and the demands of the high school he or she has attended. As both Richard Steele at Duke and Rae Lee Siporin at UCLA point out, the easy way out is not the best. Colleges do not expect students to dabble in a lot of introductory-level studies only to drop out early in the sequence. They expect them to take challenging programs. They also expect depth where there is interest. A self-proclaimed writer, for instance, should present a high school transcript that supports time and commitment in the language arts.

The high school itself counts, too. This is not to say that colleges give certain high schools preference over others. As Lawrence Groves of the University of Virginia explains, a diploma from an elite private school is no longer a guarantee of admission to a highly selective college. Nevertheless, your child's guidance office sends a school profile with all college applications it processes. From these profiles— as well as from years of experience in the field—admission people get a sense of the diversity, range, and challenge of the courses offered and the programs available at different high schools.

Along with grades, course work, and the profile of the school your child attended, admission officers will look at letters of recommendation from teachers and counselors. Though these letters only supplement the transcript itself, they do contribute to the portrait of your child as a student. Anthony Strickland of the University of North Carolina at Chapel Hill tells you what recommendations appeal to the harassed, misanthropic admission officer buried under a pile of application folders. Your child is well advised to request letters from teachers or counselors who know enough about him or her to write something substantive.

Just a word to those parents who by now have thrown up their hands and decided to help their child look into military enlistment or beauty college: Students who get A's tend to feel that grades are more valid than students who get C's, but if your child's high school record has not been an accurate reflection of his or her abilities, all is not lost. Certainly the most selective schools, as you'll learn from Linda Davis Taylor, are unlikely to overlook a poor academic performance. However, some schools will forgive those students who took a while to find themselves or get serious. One semester of stellar grades after three years of fooling around isn't the ticket to acceptance, but there are many good colleges that have time to cultivate a few late bloomers.

Whatever your child's academic history, if there needs to be a word of explanation about a dip in grades, a temporary distraction, a time of stress, or an illness, be sure to include this information prominently in the college application. If the essay isn't the place for an explanation, write a separate statement, short but to the point, and attach it to the application. If a divorce, hospitalization, or *significant* problem distracted your child in a given high school semester or if there is an explanation for uneven grades, include it. However, make sure the information your child sends is *relevant*. Philip Smith of Williams College tells how colleges react to tons of extra material in applications. There is no way around the importance of the high school record, but colleges do want the whole picture.

DUKE UNIVERSITY

> "Our child is not a straight A
> student. Just how important are grades
> and how good do they have to be?"

Richard Steele
Director of Undergraduate Admission

Many students and parents approach the college selection process with the mistaken idea that, more than any other factor, results on standardized tests will shape an admission decision. In fact, however, when an application is reviewed by a college's admission committee, the high school transcript commands the most attention. Why?

First, admission officers know that success or lack of success in college is often closely linked to a student's *attitude* toward academic work. What evidence is there of self-discipline, drive, follow-through, and sustained effort? Recommendations provide some help in revealing a student's attitude, but the transcript contains the most convincing evidence that a student has developed a good attitude toward study. For many of us at highly selective colleges, attitude is even more important than aptitude.

Second, any college admission office worth its salt regularly conducts research (usually called validity studies) to determine what best predicts success at its institution. With very few exceptions, high school performance (measured by class rank or grade point average

115

and usually weighted for more demanding course work) emerges as the top predictor of college success.

It is no wonder then that, when an admission officer comes to an applicant's transcript, out comes the magnifying glass. Most students assume that the first thing we do at this point is to examine the grades themselves. We may glance at them, but first we examine the school profile to determine as much as we can about the educational environment. How demanding is the program of study? Is advanced placement or honors work available? How tough is the competition within this school? How much grade inflation prevails there? What percentage of the seniors go on to four-year colleges? Is class rank weighted for advanced placement or honors work? If not, most highly selective colleges will consider class rank to be meaningless.

Did this particular candidate select the most demanding program possible? Did he or she have a challenging senior course sequence? If the answer to either question is no, the candidate may quickly drop out of the running at many highly selective schools. At Duke, we consider this to be so important that we evaluate every candidate on the overall quality of program as well as on actual performance within that program. If pressed, most admission officers will confess that they would rather see B's in advanced placement courses than A's in less challenging classes. However, as Bill Elliot, vice-president of enrollment planning at Carnegie Mellon University, says, "There is absolutely nothing wrong with getting A's in those advanced placement courses, either."

To what extent do we try to match up a student's program of study with a potential college major? We probably don't do this as much as most people expect. In the first place, many of the best applicants who apply to arts and sciences programs are undecided about a specific major when they apply. Since most liberal arts programs of study encourage students to explore many disciplines before selecting a major, it would be counterproductive to pay too much attention to a student's tentative major. Second, most college students change their minds three or four times before finally selecting a major. Under the circumstances, it would be foolhardy to devote a great deal of time to matching a student's tentative goals with high school preparation. But there are some important exceptions to this rule, which I should mention.

Students who are aiming at engineering or a highly specialized field of study such as physical therapy, forestry, and the like should not be surprised if members of the admission committee spend a great deal of time examining performance in subjects that are closely linked with the college major. As you might expect, we pay a great deal of attention to an applicant's performance in algebra, geometry, calculus, chemistry, and physics if that student is applying to the School of Engineering. You will find that colleges and universities are usually very open about describing the academic background necessary for success in a particular major. This information is included in view books under the selection entitled "Requirements for Admission."

It seems to me that one of the toughest issues facing the parents of a bright student who applies to a highly selective college is deciding how much nudging your son or daughter needs in selecting a demanding high school course of study. This issue must be faced each time your child is required to register for high school courses, and your advice must be tailored to the child's situation as he or she progresses. For example, you know that in order to be considered seriously by Yale, MIT, or Stanford, your teenager must elect the most challenging program available.

What should you do if your son or daughter works very hard in such courses and just barely gets C's? It seems to me that the education he or she is receiving at the moment is more important than anything else. The United States is loaded with great colleges and universities, not all of which are extremely competitive. Finding the right balance between providing excellent support and advice without creating a damaging form of pressure is one of the great challenges of parenthood. If in doubt about what to do, make sure you meet with your son's or daughter's counselor and the teachers who know your teenager best. Together you can discover the best way to encourage your son or daughter to reach his or her full potential.

Duke University is a four-year private university for men and women, located in Durham, North Carolina.

We Don't Need More Broccoli!

Rae Lee Siporin
Director of Undergraduate Admission
University of California, Los Angeles

A t UCLA, we look hard at our applicants' high school programs. We are looking for risk takers. When we evaluate an application, we want to see sustained progress in certain sensitive disciplines that prepare students for college work. Substantive work in English, math, science, four years of a language, advanced placement courses, courses at the local community college stand out. Two years of the easiest foreign language, a little math in tenth grade, another math course as a senior is playing it safe. Kids who "veg" through high school and just take the minimum, the easy A's, aren't going to rise to the challenge of becoming risk takers in college. A selective institution doesn't have the luxury of allowing for a lot of late bloomers. We don't need more broccoli; we need students who are the best prepared.

UNIVERSITY OF VIRGINIA

> ## "Our child went to a public high school. Do students from private schools have an edge in the application process?"

Lawrence A. Groves
Associate Dean of Admission

The conversation is familiar, usually taking place in April in college admission offices around the country. The college counselor at a private school is calling about an applicant who was denied admission. Expressing disbelief (if not shock) at the decision, the counselor rattles off the applicant's qualities, with an emphasis on her high SAT scores. The admission dean listens patiently, acknowledging the attributes of the applicant but finally noting that she places no higher than the middle of the class (not always easy to determine since few private schools provide rank-in-class information) and her performance lacks the distinction for admission to the college. The counselor quickly reminds the dean about the stiff academic competition at his school. He points out that the applicant got straight A's at a public high school and would have been right at the top of her class had she not transferred to private school. The admission dean, though sympathetic to the counselor's argument, says there is nothing he can do. The issue is her performance in the context of her current academic environ-

119

ment, not something from the past or speculation about what might have been, and she does not qualify on this basis. The counselor persists, emphasizing the strength of the school, the excellent students, and so forth, until it becomes apparent to the dean that the counselor is not so much an advocate for an applicant as he is for his school. The conversation finally ends, amicably. Unknown to the dean, the counselor has other calls to make to colleges where his applicant has been denied or placed on the waiting list.

This conversation highlights a change in the strong link that has historically existed between selective colleges and private schools. Two to three decades ago, mere attendance at one of the elite private schools such as Exeter, Andover, Groton, or Choate virtually assured a student admission to almost any prestigious college. Many other good private schools could also expect their share of acceptances to the top colleges. Today, however, the percentage of private school students enrolled in selective colleges has dropped. Where 50 to 60 percent of students once came from the private sector, most of the top colleges now enroll no more than 20 to 30 percent.

Are the private schools seeing a drop in the quality of their students? Has the academic excellence associated with private schools slipped? The answer probably is no to both questions. Private schools appear to be as strong as they have ever been. Instead, the change has taken place at the college level, generated by the events of the sixties and seventies when colleges began to seek greater diversity in their student bodies. Coeducation, affirmative action, and efforts to attract students from different geographic regions altered college enrollments. Students from public high schools also discovered the Ivy League colleges that had traditionally favored the private school graduate.

Another phenomenon has further diminished the influence that private schools once exerted in the college admission process. There has been an increasing interest shown by students in gaining admission to the top colleges ("hot" colleges in some circles). Numbering about a hundred, these colleges include the Ivy League schools (regular and "little"), Duke, Stanford, Carleton, Swarthmore, Northwestern, and so on, plus a few public universities such as Berkeley, Michigan, North Carolina, and Virginia. By and large, these colleges have chosen not to increase enrollment during a time when applications have been steadily increasing. If Andover had a mythical twenty "slots" at an

Ivy League school ten years ago, that number has not increased (and may have decreased), but the number of applications to the college has gone up. In an absolute sense, there is no question that private school students no longer have a pipeline to the top colleges. And outside the elite group, it is a struggle for independents to place more than a handful of their students in these colleges.

One might deduce that these changes have made it easier for public high school students to get into the selective colleges and, in a certain sense, this is true—perhaps not easier, but the public schools now provide these colleges with a wealth of talent that went untapped not too many years ago. As a result, elite public high schools in the affluent suburbs of most major metropolitan areas are believed to be stepping-stones to selective colleges. No doubt, real estate agents can probably tell you how many National Merit semifinalists there were and who went to Harvard, Yale, and Princeton in the current year from the local schools. This is probably less a function of the schools and more directly related to the fact that both parents have college degrees (perhaps advanced degrees) and an income that puts them in the highest tax bracket. Still, students from top public high schools are in greater demand. The recruiting efforts of the selective colleges focus on these schools, and their representatives will make individual visits as well as attend college-night programs.

Though the relationship between selective colleges and private and public schools has changed, most admission officers will stress that they admit *students*, not schools. This is a safe statement with an element of truth, but the reality is that schools *do* count in the admission process to selective colleges. In the private sector, the high school will become a strong and active advocate for its applicants. Much more than the public school counselor, the private school counselor knows that part of his or her school's image is inextricably linked to the colleges where its students matriculate. Though one might argue about the term *prep school*, parents are not spending the money they do just to see the school disregard the placement of their children into the best colleges that will accept them. Private school counselors are usually on a first-name basis with admission people in the selective colleges; public school counselors rarely ever call, and if they do, it is usually after an admission decision (typically about a denied student) has been made. Private school counselors often call before the decisions go out and attempt to move marginal candidates onto the acceptance list. Interestingly, Stanford (almost alone among top colleges) refuses to discuss admission decisions with counselors before they are made, thus avoiding the gentle arm-twisting.

What is the relationship between schools and colleges likely to be in the next few years? It is probable that the selective colleges will move closer to the ideal of admitting students instead of schools. It appears that selectivity in admission to these top colleges will remain high and may well increase. They will seek the most talented students, and it is unlikely that any one or group of schools will have an advantage. With the college-going rate increasing, selective colleges will have many more places to find top students. The result will be great for the colleges, but some independent and public secondary schools may lose ground in the favored relationship they have enjoyed with colleges.

The University of Virginia is a four-year public university for men and women, located in Charlottesville, Virginia.

AMHERST COLLEGE

"How do highly selective colleges make their decisions about applicants, and why do they seem at times unfair?"

Linda Davis Taylor
Dean of Admission

It is the middle of March, and the members of the admission committee (eight deans of admission, two members of the faculty, and two students) are involved in a long discussion about a candidate's application. The staff member who handles this region of the country is speaking about the case:

"This young man will be the valedictorian of his graduating class of 450. He comes with enthusiastic recommendations from the school counselors and teachers, one of whom says 'he's one of the finest writers I've seen in a dozen years of teaching.' He hasn't held any significant position of leadership, but he has been a member of several clubs, plays varsity soccer, and has traveled widely in the summers. He's a fine pianist and the evaluation of his audition with our music department suggests that he could be a strong contributor there—they'd love to have him. The soccer coach says he's a good possibility down the road. I vote to admit."

"I disagree," says another committee member. "He may be number one in his class now, but he isn't doing as well in his senior year. Though his school offers additional honors courses, which he could have taken this year, he chose to take a couple of electives instead of advanced placement courses. His grades and scores look good, but after reading his essays, I disagree with the English teacher who says that he's a fine writer. In *our* context he could certainly do the work, but I don't see anything about his application that really stands out. We'll have other good soccer players and pianists recommended to us that we'll be more excited about. I say deny admission."

As the votes are taken, this strong student is not admitted. Needless to say, when he receives the decision, he and his parents will wonder what more he could have done to improve his application.

In recent years, many highly selective colleges have seen their applicant pools grow ever larger, despite earlier warnings of declining numbers of college-age students. Larger applicant pools combined with efforts to achieve greater diversity in entering classes have made the admission process seem more mysterious than ever to prospective students and their parents.

To better understand the process, consider some of the issues facing the admission office of a highly selective college. Generally, the admission office has the responsibility of implementing the college's overall admission policy, including general admission requirements, required high school courses, and standardized tests, but the individual decisions are left to the judgment of the committee that actually reads the applications. The college trustees, faculty, and administration often articulate the overall mission of the college so that parents and students can better understand the kinds of students who might best profit from the college's academic program and environment. Highly selective colleges usually have great interest in enrolling a class with a broad socioeconomic, ethnic, geographic, and personal diversity. Rarely will you find these policies written in the form of specific numbers, but the admission dean knows all the constituencies that need to be represented in the entering class. When the freshman class arrives each fall, the college hopes both that the class will be academically and intellectually exciting and that it will include students who will contribute to campus life—arts, athletics, clubs, and organizations. Later the college hopes that most students will not only graduate but also go on to make some significant contribution to their families, communities, and perhaps even society at large. Making judgments about students that will bring about these kinds of achievements seems like a tall order.

Perhaps it's obvious, but it should certainly be stated again: A highly selective college denies admission to students who are as well qualified as those it admits. Often the decision to admit or deny is based on the subjective views of the individuals reading an application. In a highly selective college, it is rarely possible for each admission staff member to read *all* the applications. Subcommittees are formed so that each file can be read by several different people. The full admission committee considers only those candidates who are evaluated as the strongest by the subcommittees. In making each final decision, the committee listens to the ratings given by the readers, discusses the components of the student's file, and weighs carefully the pros and cons of offering one of its slots to each student as he or she is presented. The individual components of the file that are evaluated include:

- **High school record.** Both the grade point average and the quality of the secondary school program are considered. Did the student take the most challenging courses available and have a stable record of performance?
- **Recommendations.** Do the counselor and teachers stand behind the student? Are there specific comments that identify the student as intellectually exciting or gifted in a particular academic area?
- **Test scores.** Many students who apply to highly selective colleges are good testers (and others manage to improve their scores by taking prep courses!). Highly selective colleges have high median and mean test scores, but they also look for individuals whose talents and potential are not accurately reflected by standardized testing. *Strong test scores alone do not guarantee admission, and low test scores don't preclude it.*
- **Essays.** The candidate's essays provide the all-important "sparkle" to the file. Without this sparkle, application folders become frighteningly similar collections of transcripts and test scores. Essays not only help the admission committee to evaluate the candidate's communication skills but also provide some insight into personal characteristics. Ad-

125

mission committees are not looking for the "right" or necessarily the most clever answer to a question. Students who come across well are those who write well and who are sincere. Too many candidates make their applications look like résumés. By "packaging" themselves, they cover up what we really want to see—the qualities that set them apart from others.

☐ **Activities.** Students often think that they should have a long list of activities on their applications. Not true. Admission officers are more interested in candidates who have pursued a few interests in depth than in those who have dabbled in many. Special skills and talents will be noted and, in some cases, may help to sway the committee's vote.

Once the committee makes decisions about all of the individual applicants, the admission office examines the overall "profile" of the admitted class to be certain that the class as a whole represents the kind of academic and personal diversity that will create an exciting and stimulating campus environment. Final decisions at highly selective colleges are difficult. Though none of us can claim to be perfect, we do think that we complete our evaluations thoroughly and with great care and concern for the individuals behind the paper.

Amherst College is a four-year private liberal arts college for men and women, located in Amherst, Massachusetts.

UNIVERSITY OF NORTH CAROLINA AT CHAPEL HILL

> ## "How important are the recommendations of teachers and counselors? Will they affect our child's chances of acceptance at college?"

Anthony R. Strickland
Associate Director of Admission

The good ones come flooding back:

> She is a fine student, aggressive, courageous, with great insight and a fine store of low cunning. She is a strong, compassionate, imaginative senior proctor, and she was captain of a field hockey team this fall that has gone undefeated for two years.

The anecdotes that followed smacked of hyperbole and, by the time I got to the last paragraph, I was salivating freely and feeling that I would be somehow less a human being if I never met the person about whom this recommendation had been written.

> So I give you, with my most fervent endorsement, a bright, creative, industrious, involved, funny, compassionate, beautiful girl.

127

She desperately wants to go South to college and North Carolina is her first choice. Somehow, it just doesn't seem possible to me that you might not want her desperately, and I shall be terribly sorry to lose her fine influence.

So we admitted her. And she went to college somewhere else.

The recurrence of examples such as this one could have conditioned me to an unbecoming cynicism about recommendations in general had there not been myriad others, perhaps less insightful, perhaps less well written, that nonetheless communicated something very important about the subject. Some teachers and counselors can write well and some cannot. Some college admission officers are literate, compassionate, and insightful, able to read between the lines of a recommendation and make a considered, rational decision, as humane as the circumstances will permit. I myself am that way about five days out of the reading year, when I can interpret anything that I read to the gratification and often wonderment of those who are writing. On the 283 other reading days when I am not this way, a writer is well advised to consider that I am harassed, misanthropic, and certain in the expectation that, when Friday comes, I can only look forward to reading application folders over the weekend.

What recommendations appeal under these circumstances?

First, anecdotes are much better than strings of adjectives and adverbs. In the first week of reading applications, an admission staff sees every adjective and adverb in the English language, as well as in several foreign languages, and the words rapidly cease to have any meaning. To understand them, I need examples. Since I am unfamiliar with the person being written about, some sort of composite of observations by teachers, athletic coaches, drama coaches, or others in the school with *specific* knowledge of tangible accomplishment is my only resource. This is the philosophy behind recommendations in the first place, since it is rarely possible for one person to know everything a student has been up to in and out of class. Your child should request recommendations from writers who know him or her thoroughly.

Second, truth is much better than falsehood. I cannot agree with Robert Pirsig's observation in *Zen and the Art of Motorcycle Maintenance* that people have an innate capacity for recognizing quality when they encounter it. I do know, however, that people have an innate capacity for recognizing falseness when they come across it. If a recommendation presents someone as something he or she is not, readers very quickly pick up on that. I sympathize deeply with counselors when they are called upon to write a recommendation for the basic "nice kid" who has no outstanding qualities but who is the sort of person that makes the school run. I have come to the conclusion that in these cases it is best to say, "So-and-so is the basic nice kid," and let it go at that. Don't expect the recommendation writer to embroider the facts.

Third, fresh is much better than stale. Patterns of evaluating, writing, or phrasing are especially obvious when a number of applications to an individual college or university come from one school. Often, these applications are read as a group in order to ensure some consistency, and the repetition of various phrases or observations is readily apparent. To avoid stale recommendations, your child might want to meet with teachers and counselors shortly before they write their letters so that they have a fresh impression to draw from.

Fourth, remember that recommendations are only part of the total application picture and that applicants must be counted upon to do certain things for themselves. Parents have a tendency to blame teachers and counselors when their child is not accepted at a chosen college ("What exactly *did* you say about our child?"). More likely than not, however, the admission personnel at the college discovered some deficiency in record or involvement on the child's application before the recommendations even had a chance to influence their decision. You and your child must realize—and keep reminding yourselves— that you cannot suddenly make a lack of intellectual aggressiveness attractive, nor can you suddenly change modest involvement in the life of the school and community into an impressive record of extracurricular achievement. Obviously you will worry about these things. You will awaken at 2:00 A.M., and, before rolling over to try to go back to sleep, you will wonder if you should have made your child do and be more or different things. Again, I assure you that a specific term or phrase in a description of tangible accomplishments is perhaps one one-thousandth of the total consideration given to an applicant and, from my own coldly objective standpoint, should not be a source of worry. *I* will occasionally awaken at 2:00 A.M., wonder if I have been consistent or if I have followed through a particular case as far as I should have, and then make my own attempt to go back to sleep.

And teachers and counselors themselves engage in a little early morning soul-searching about whether or not they are doing a complete and perfect job. You can believe in the conscientiousness both of those speaking on behalf of your child and of those reading on his or her behalf.

Fifth, counselors cannot be "brokers" for your child. Often in the course of a year, and as counselor–admission officer relations develop, I may be able to spare a school embarrassment because of an administrative glitch, and a counselor, through a thoughtful letter or phone call, may be able to save me some embarrassment because of something our readers overlooked. In the short run, it is tempting to believe that requests for special consideration from the standpoint of "I just did this for you, now you immediately do this for me" can be made. This is not pleasant for any one and often puts either the admission counselor or the school counselor in an untenable position. Over the years, however, a relationship based on mutual concern and trust makes it possible for special phone calls to be made about an individual case that is causing some local problems. When a particular class has many more National Merit semifinalists, or persons with "96" averages, or whatever, than previous classes, some special pleading may be appropriate; however, I can assure you that if every class is the best that ever went through the school, any admission staff will soon begin to question a counselor's credibility. Do not expect your child's counselor to champion your son or daughter in a good old boy network.

Sixth, encourage your child to present himself or herself as well as possible on the application. The recommendation writers are important but they cannot be expected to know everything about every person about whom they write. Realize early—and keep reminding yourself—that recommendations are only a part of the whole application-admitting-enrolling procedure and that several paragraphs of terse epigrammatic prose cannot compensate for individual shortcomings in academics or other types of achievement. The applicant must stand or fall on his or her own merits. Make sure *your child* makes a good case. Support letters can only *support*.

Finally, our staff can be accommodating and flexible for an occasional person who seems to exemplify all that is good and worthwhile about a school. We cannot do it every year, nor can we admit the special person each year who has helped the counseling office run smoothly or who has served as a spark plug for the field hockey team.

Unfortunately, every year I encounter several dozen applicants who would have been admitted had the remaining members of my staff been astute enough to see what I saw in the particular candidate. They probably feel the same way about me sometimes, although I have not asked them. In any event, we all do the best we can to give recommendations as much credence as possible. However, we are all limited by circumstance and often cannot do the things that *we* think best, in spite of the greatest caring and concern.

The University of North Carolina at Chapel Hill is a four-year public university for men and women, located in Chapel Hill, North Carolina.

WILLIAMS COLLEGE

"Does it help to send extra material
with the college application?"

Philip F. Smith
Director of Admission

When our admission committee considers supplementary materials in a candidate's application folder, we are attracted to information that adds substantively to our knowledge of the candidate. Basically, we subscribe to the "three D" approach to college applications: describe, document, and detail. Information that further describes what a candidate has done or that documents or adds detail to a candidate's achievements is always valuable.

Over the years, several types of additional support material have been helpful to our admission committee. Every year we receive enough tapes of musical performances to fill several bushel baskets. We send the full baskets to the music department, and each tape is reviewed by a faculty member. The resulting evaluation is placed in the student's folder, which is read by three members of our committee. The three readers value the extra documentation, as does the full committee when it takes up the folder during decision time in March.

Any other evidence of talent or unusual achievement that we receive—artwork, videotapes of dramatic performances, athletic films and times, samples of creative writing, special term papers, published scientific articles—is treated in the same way. It is sent to the appro-

132

priate department for review, and the evaluation is placed in the student's folder. Like tapes of musical performances, most of this material adds to our knowledge of a candidate and is therefore valued by our admission committee. Let me emphasize, however, that the material must be both exceptional and relevant to the academic or extracurricular goals of the candidate.

In addition to evidence of talent or achievement, each year we also receive numerous letters of recommendation or explanation from sources outside normal school channels. Some of these we value; most we do not. Among the letters that we occasionally find helpful are these:

☐ Letters from employers that describe how well a candidate has fulfilled work responsibilities. Letters of this type are especially beneficial for potential work-study students.

☐ Letters from supervisors of volunteer or social service organizations that detail a student's involvement. If the involvement has been extensive, these letters can provide insights into how the student has contributed to or gained from the experience.

☐ Letters from medical personnel that document a major health problem that a student has encountered in secondary school. Especially if the secondary school is not fully aware of the problem, letters of this type can add greatly to our understanding of the circumstances the student has been facing. Again, though, the circumstances must be truly significant or unusual.

☐ Letters from peers that give us a sense of how a candidate uses time or what kind of friend he or she is. For the past fifteen years, applicants to Williams have been asked for a peer reference from a contemporary who knows them well. I have been uniformly impressed with the candid, responsible, and helpful way in which peer recommenders have written references for their friends.

Among the letters that we rarely find helpful are general letters of endorsement from assorted influential people and letters of recommendation from private counselors or independent educational consultants. Letters from alumni endorsing a candidate's family are fairly prevalent. These letters often begin with the disclaimer "I don't really know the candidate, but if he or she is anything like the family, then he or she is marvelous." We always politely acknowledge this information, but it almost never adds anything substantive to the candidate's folder or to our assessment of his or her qualifications. The same is true of generic letters of endorsement from politicians and other prominent citizens.

When we receive what appears to be an orchestrated barrage of such letters for one candidate, the overall effect can be modestly negative. If a number of similar letters from alumni, prominent people, and various unconnected personages appear in a folder, I have noticed that our committee members feel as if they are being manipulated, and they have to fight a little harder to remain objective.

Letters from private counselors or independent educational consultants are met with equal skepticism. Since these people are basically paid advocates for their clients, our committee members are automatically suspicious of their letters and tend not to read them when they are included in a candidate's folder. During the past three years, I cannot cite a single instance in which a letter from a private counselor or independent educational consultant made a significant difference for a candidate or caused the committee to change its decision.

Besides the letters and supplementary materials that we regularly receive at Williams, we occasionally get miscellaneous other items that are of no value whatsoever to our admission committee. For instance, because our school mascot is a purple cow, applicants sometimes send us purple cow gifts—knitted scarves, hats, pictures of themselves attired in purple cow clothing. One year an applicant also sent us a three-foot-tall, twenty-five-foot-long computer banner that said, "Don't forget (student's name)." We didn't forget the student; in fact, we hung the banner in the admission staff room, where it served as a constant reminder. However, we didn't admit the student, either!

In general, extra material in a student's folder that adds relevant new information beyond the data presented by the candidate and by the school can be helpful. Extraneous information is usually politely filed and does not carry any weight in our decisions. Best of all, material that adds at least one of the "three D's" is gratefully considered.

Williams College is a four-year private liberal arts college for men and women, located in Williamstown, Massachusetts.

The Common Application: What Is It and How Does It Work?

The pressure, stress, and burden of filing six or eight different applications is something colleges as well as parents dread. Twelve years ago, several private colleges across the country decided to develop what they agreed upon as a "common" college application. Today 117 colleges accept the Common Application (see next page), either exclusively or in place of their own application, and every two years they meet to review and improve the form to suit their admission needs.

As a group, these colleges make up the Common Application Office, which is located in the offices of the National Association of Secondary School Principals (NASSP) in Reston, Virginia. NASSP acts as the Common Application Office's agent and distributes the Common Application to all high schools.

The four-page Common Application has several advantages for both students and the colleges that accept it. Application deadlines and fee requirements are enclosed with the form so students can quickly find this information for all participating colleges. Students need to complete the form only once; then they may photocopy it for other participating colleges they are applying to. High school counselors can use the form to help sophomores and juniors learn about applying to colleges.

Students should check with their high school guidance counselors, look at the Common Application form, and see if any of the colleges they are thinking of applying to are members of the Common Application Office.

FIFTY COLLEGE ADMISSION DIRECTORS SPEAK TO PARENTS

Agnes Scott ● Alfred ● Allegheny ● American University ● Antioch ● Bard College ● Bates ● Beloit ● Bennington ● Boston University ● Brandeis ● Bryn Mawr ● Bucknell ● Carleton ● Case Western Reserve ● Centenary College of Louisiana ● Centre College ● Claremont McKenna ● Clark University ● Coe Colby-Sawyer ● Colgate ● Colorado College ● Denison ● University of Denver ● DePauw ● Dickinson ● Drew ● Eartham ● Eckerd ● Elmira ● Emery Fairfield ● Fisk ● Fordham ● Franklin & Marshall ● Furman ● Gettysburg ● Goucher ● Grinnell ● Guilford ● Hamilton ● Hampden-Sydney ● Hampshire Hartwick ● Haverford ● Hobart ● Hood

Lawrence ● Lehigh ● Lewis and Clark ● Linfield **COMMON APPLICATION**

Mills ● Millsaps ● Morehouse ● Mount University ● Oberlin ● Occidental ● Ohio Puget Sound ● Randolph-Macon ● Randolph Redlands ● Reed ● Rhodes ● Rice

Kalamazoo ● Kenyon ● Knox ● Lafayette
Macalester ● Manhattan ● Manhattanville
Holyoke ● Muhlenberg ● New York
Wesleyan ● Pitzer ● Pomona ● University of
Macon Woman's College ● University of
University of Richmond ● Ripon ● University

of Rochester ● Rollins ● St. Lawrence ● St. Olaf ● Salem ● Sarah Lawrence ● Scripps ● Simmons ● Skidmore ● Smith ● University of the South University of Southern California ● Southern Methodist ● Spelman ● Stetson ● Susquehanna ● Swarthmore ● Texas Christian University Trinity College ● Trinity University ● Tulane ● Union ● Valparaiso ● Vanderbilt ● Vassar ● Wake Forest ● Washington College ● Washington and Lee ● Wells ● Wesleyan ● Western Maryland ● Wheaton ● Whitman ● Willamette ● William Smith ● Williams ● Wooster ● Worcester Polytechnic

APPLICATION FOR UNDERGRADUATE ADMISSION

The colleges and universities listed above encourage the use of this application. No distinction will be made between it and the college's own form. The accompanying instructions tell you how to complete, copy, and file your application to any one or several of the colleges. Please type or print in black ink.

PERSONAL DATA

Legal name: _____

      Last   *First*   *Middle (complete)*   *Jr., etc.*   *Sex*

Prefer to be called: _____(nickname)   Former last name(s) if any: _____

Are you applying as a □ freshman or □ transfer student?   For the term beginning: _____

Permanent home address: _____

                    Number and Street

     City or Town   *County*   *State*   *Zip .*

If different from the above, please give your mailing address for all admission correspondence:

Mailing address: _____

                    Number and Street

     City or Town   *State*   *Zip*

Telephone at mailing address: _____ / _____ Permanent home telephone: _____ / _____

            Area Code   *Number*   *Area Code*   *Number*

Birthdate: _____ Citizenship: □ U.S. □ Permanent Resident U.S. □ Other _____ Visa type _____

   Month Day Year   *Country*

Possible area(s) of academic concentration/major: _____ or undecided □

Special college or division if applicable: _____

Possible career or professional plans: _____ or undecided □

Will you be a candidate for financial aid?   Yes _____   No _____   If yes, the appropriate form(s) was/will

be filed on: _____

The following items are optional:

Social Security number, if any: □ □ □ □ □ □ □ □ □

Place of birth: _____ Marital status: _____ Height: _____ Weight: _____

     City   *State*   *Country*

Parents' country of birth: Mother _____ Father _____

What is your first language, if other than English? _____

How would you describe yourself: (Please check one)
□ American Indian or Alaskan Native   □ Hispanic (including Puerto Rican)
□ Asian or Pacific Islander (including Indian subcontinent)   □ White, Anglo, Caucasian (non-Hispanic)
□ Black (non-Hispanic)   □ Other (Specify)

EDUCATIONAL DATA

School you attend now _____ ACT/CEEB code number _____

Address _____

            City   *State*   *Zip Code*

Date of secondary graduation _____ Is your school public? _____ private? _____ parochial? _____

College advisor: _____ School telephone: _____ / _____

         Name   *Position*   *Area Code*   *Number*

                                                  APP

Reprinted with the kind permission of the Common Application Office, NASSP, Reston, Virginia.

136

The Elusive College Essay

"Writing is easy: All you do is sit staring at a blank sheet of paper until the drops of blood form on your forehead."

—GENE FOWLER

As competition at the most selective colleges increases, the search for a winning edge intensifies. Each part of the application has had a moment in the limelight. Test scores, for example, were a hot issue several years ago. Recently, attention has shifted to the application essay. The change in focus has given rise to a number of books and articles on how to turn a question like "Do you have any heroes?" (Bowdoin) or a directive like "Please attach a photograph of something that has special meaning for you" (Vassar) into an effective essay. It has also given rise to a couple of unfortunate myths about the application essay that should be dispelled at once.

The first myth is that certain topics are "bad" or "wrong." Counselors often steer their seniors away from hackneyed subjects like the trip to France, the summer in Israel, the divorce, the team, the twin. True, these topics are not original; many essays are written on them, or subjects like them, every year. It's not the topic, however, that makes an application essay effective or ineffective; it's the treatment of the topic that counts. A young person who has been engaged in and genuinely affected by an experience, no matter how mundane, can write a strong creative essay about it. The key is to maintain a sincere, enthusiastic tone and to include enough details to allow the reader to share in the experience. So if your daughter chooses a less than original topic, don't wince. Instead, encourage her to take the topic and make it specifically and vividly her own. (Do offer to do a little proofreading, though. An essay about a summer spent in a "youth hostile" is doomed from the start!)

The second myth goes hand in hand with the first. It says that, since the usual topics are too predictable, only essays that astonish, amuse, or amaze can get students in. "Did you hear who got into Harvard? His essay was about candy! He made them a *veritas* shield out of chocolate!" The notion that only high-impact originality will win an admission officer's approval is as misguided as the belief that conventional topics are unacceptable in and of themselves. In the first place, as the admission professionals make clear, the application essay alone cannot get a student into college. In the second place, since few people, let alone seventeen-year-olds, are capable of matching the caliber, intensity, and style demanded by the high-risk essay, this approach is more likely to fail than succeed. In the third place, though originality is certainly an asset, it is not the only quality that colleges look for in prospective students. For these reasons, it is advisable to discourage your son from being eccentric simply to make an impression. Admission counselors may just remember his essay as the most inappropriate—or the most embarrassing!

In this chapter, William T. Conley of Drew University offers some tips on how to approach the application essay, Theodore O'Neill of the University of Chicago explains why colleges require it, and Karl M. Furstenberg of Wesleyan University in Connecticut and John Bunnell of Stanford talk about the essay in relation to the other components of a student's application folder. They all agree that the essay personalizes the admission process. If taken seriously and written honestly, it gives them a glimpse of the human being behind the grades and the test scores. They also agree that the essay should be consistent with the other parts of the application and should contribute to a sense of the whole person. The pieces of the puzzle, in other words, should all fit together.

"Wrong" topics? Not really. For a voice major, an essay on the school musical not only is appropriate but may very well be more engaging and revealing than an essay on some unusual subject. "Right" topics? Forget it. No one can second-guess a group as diverse as most admission committees. The best advice for the essay is "Stand up straight and believe in yourself." As William Hiss at Bates College says, "We don't want the back lot of MGM, a created scene over a barren field. We want to see the real landscape."

DREW UNIVERSITY

> "Our daughter is ready to write
> college application essays but needs
> some basic advice on how to begin.
> Where should she start?"

William T. Conley
Director of Admission

Honestly, there was a time not so very long ago when applying to college was a reasonably straightforward process. In those halcyon days the prospective college applicant would consult a guidance counselor, research a manageable number of college reference guides, discuss the options with his or her parents, visit several campuses, and then apply to fewer than half a dozen schools. This scenario was familiar as recently as the 1970s but seems antediluvian given today's college admission climate. A guidance counselor is now only one of many consulted, the proliferation of college reference materials can do more to confuse than to clarify, the role of parents is in constant transition, and the student often reacts to this complexity by applying to more than nine or ten colleges.

This dramatic change, from a simple process to a complex rite of passage, is especially evident in how much emphasis is now placed on the individual components of applying to college. Standardized test preparation courses are crowded, students are arranging practice interviews, parents are arguing class rank policies, and publishers are coming out with specialized books on how to write winning application essays. Although I am reluctant to fuel this obsession with the parts— rather than concern for the whole—I also see the value of putting the essay in perspective and helping your son or daughter prepare one that is well written and compelling.

First and foremost, admission to a competitive college rests on no single factor. Decisions are made by integrating three general areas: school record, standardized testing (if required), and personal qualities. Individual colleges will place varying degrees of importance on each area for each student. The application essay is primarily intended to help admission officers "flesh out" the applicant's personal side. It is generally safe to say that a good or bad essay *cannot* be singularly responsible for admission or denial. However, the essay *can* play a significant role in strengthening or weakening a candidacy.

In recognizing the essay for what it is—a part of a more important whole—a student can approach it with less fear and trembling. The first thing to do is to read through each application to determine the number and nature of the essays required. This initial exercise will give the student a realistic sense of the time needed to complete the entire application and the subjects the essays should address. Perhaps the most common cause of a poorly written essay is failure to anticipate the preparation time needed to organize thoughts and place them on paper. It can't all be done in a single Sunday afternoon. Another basic problem can be selecting an inappropriate topic or misconstruing the prescribed one. The way to avoid these problems is simple: Allow time to think and write!

In many cases, colleges allow flexibility in selecting a subject for the essay. It can be helpful if the student identifies important people, events, and ideas in his or her life. These can lead to stimulating essay topics. The student should bounce possible topics off friends, parents, siblings, or teachers. I recall a wonderful essay written in response to the question "What book has had the most significant impact on you and why?" This essay was not about *A Catcher in the Rye* or *The Grapes of Wrath*, but about the inspirational power of *The Little Engine That Could*. Once the student has some exciting possibilities, he or she can consider creative ways to approach them. Often an impediment to this personalized approach is a student's concern with "what *they* want to read." Admission officers want to read what *students* want to write.

Even when restricted to a prescribed subject, the student should

141

recognize the potential for creative responses. For several years, the Common Application offered an essay option in which students could choose an important person from the past and conduct an imaginary interview. The usual candidates would be rounded up—Abraham Lincoln, Jesus Christ, Adolf Hitler, among others—but one student interpreted *important* in a more personal, direct way. He interviewed his grandfather, whom he had never had an opportunity to meet. Sometimes it is appropriate to "color outside the lines" in responding to an apparently static topic.

Above all, the fundamental quality of a good essay is good writing. All the creativity in the world cannot overcome an essay that is technically flawed. The college admission officer assumes that the writer has more than pen and paper within reach. An essay marked by misspellings, misplaced punctuation, tense shifts, and plain poor style can say two very damaging things: one, that regardless of good grades or test scores, the person cannot apply academic skills to a basic exercise; two, he or she did not consider the application important and did not put forth much effort. In either case, the style can effectively sabotage well-conceived intent. A dictionary should always be within reach, and there should be no such thing as a first and final draft. Sharing the essay with a second reader who can comment objectively on its technical merit is not cheating but exhibiting good common sense.

Another characteristic of an effective essay is originality. Although the creative interpretation of an essay question may reflect originality, the actual execution may not. Perhaps the most obvious example of this is what I call "Roget's essay." Here the student uses (and frequently misuses) language that is pretentious rather than words that say it better and more genuinely. Of course some students have command of considerable vocabularies and employ them effectively. The rule of thumb is quite straightforward: Not only the content but also the style should reflect the writer's personality. When in doubt, don't reach for a thesaurus. Say it simply.

The first question students generally ask about a writing assignment is how long it should be. Unfortunately, they don't usually want to determine how fully the subject should be treated but how soon they can stop writing! This is true of the application essay as well. In some cases, the instructions will specify maximum length, but more frequently the length will be left to the student's judgment. I would recommend no more than three pages. The questions are generally designed to be answered in a focused manner, and essays must be read along with dozens of other pages of information. Economy without sacrificing content will receive kudos from the bleary-eyed application reader. The long-winded essay that rambles slowly to nowhere can leave the reader uninspired and unimpressed. While on the subject of volume, let me emphasize that a student should not submit material in gross excess of what is required. Those superfluous "writing samples" simply make the folder thicker, not more complete. A student should make his or her mark as a writer in the essays required.

Marshall McLuhan wrote that "the medium is the message," and this idea is particularly applicable to the college essay. The advantages of a creatively conceived and technically well written essay can be offset by the "medium." As well as obscuring the actual message, illegible writing, muddied type, or poor-quality paper communicates carelessness and disregard for the reader's eyes. If the essay can't be typed, it should be written neatly. If a typewriter is used, the keys should be clean. If multiple copies are made, they should all be sharp and clear. Students should remember that their applications will be handled many times and that paper designed for confetti probably won't hold up in the application review process.

Clearly, there are many elements to a well-written college essay: creativity, originality, technique, brevity, and appearance. Although the college essay is just one of many factors considered in the review of a college application, it will provide important insights into an applicant's personality and preparation for the demands of college-level writing. These are reasons enough to take the application essay seriously.

Drew University is a four-year private university for men and women, located in Madison, New Jersey.

UNIVERSITY OF CHICAGO

> "Why do kids have to write
> application essays? Our son is going
> nuts—and so are we—trying to think of
> what famous person from history he'd
> like to have lunch with!"

Theodore O'Neill
Director of College Admission

Most people involved with the college admission process agree that
too many hours are spent, too much energy is expended, and too
many tears are shed over the whole business. Everyone wishes the
process could be as humane as possible. When looking for a solution,
students, parents, and admission officers alike point to the college
application essay as the piece that is most struggled over.

Why not, then, get rid of the essay? Doing so would certainly have
a few obvious and immediate benefits. It would eliminate the all-
night bouts of writing before the deadline, the crumpled balls of
paper, the Federal Express expenses. It would allow admission officers
to spend more time with their families and friends in February and
March, when they are usually reading mountains of application essays.
Most important (and anyone who has tried to compose a "personal
statement" at any point in his or her life knows how great a benefit
this would be), it would relieve applicants of the pain of struggling

144

to reveal themselves on paper and would protect them from the risk of subjecting their self-revelations to the judgment of perfect strangers.

The question is, would eliminating the essay make the admission process more humane? And if it would, wouldn't basing everything on numbers, as some state universities find that they must, make it even more humane? Then, at least, no person would have to say no to any other person; the admission decision would be strictly impartial. (Dear Applicant: We regret that we cannot accept you for admission. Don't take this personally. Your numbers simply don't match up with our numbers.) For that matter, why not go one step further? Why not relegate admission decisions to a national computer matching service, as some people are seriously proposing? Then in the spring a student would get one thick acceptance letter and *no* thin rejection letters. Wouldn't this be the ultimate in humane responses?

The answer, of course, is no. It's ridiculous to suggest that the computerized or institutionalized response is the most humane. Philosophers have told us since the beginning of time that what is most humane is the conscious and distinctive use of language. The way to make a college application a real human affair is to model it on correspondence or, when possible, a conversation, not on a measurement. What a college needs to be able to do is to judge the whole person, and in order to do that, it needs to hear a voice that resonates with the human qualities of the academically qualified applicant. The only useful tip, then, for students who want to write proper college application essays is this: Let yourselves be heard in your writing. Don't try to ape someone else or to sound the way you think colleges want you to sound. Speak in your own voice.

Speaking in one's own voice should be easy, but we all know that it isn't. Young children, up to a certain point, always speak in their own way, and polished writers find a style that says something honest about them. The rest of us, however, have other things to wrestle with in order to get our own true selves on paper. We *can* do it—anyone can. There is a voice down there, and we know it when we hear it, but we often have to make many frustrating false starts before it emerges.

When an essay is submitted that is truly representative of the student, the college admission process begins to make sense. Since the model for application reading should be interpretation rather than measurement (because success in college relates to character and motivation much more than to things more easily gauged), the essay and interview provide the context in which to interpret everything else, such as transcripts and test scores. If a student can write with some thoughtfulness and self-knowledge, he or she is already doing much of what is asked for in college. Essay writing is taken as primary evidence of something crucial to collegiate study.

Perhaps the essay makes the whole business of applying to college more daunting, but at least in acknowledging its importance we in admission are making a pact with applicants that says, "If you sweat over the essay, we will, too. We will do *our* best to reveal ourselves to you by trying to describe our college with a voice that is distinctive and true to the institution. We will not make vague, intrusive demands ('Say something about yourself'); we will pose questions that interest us and allow you to write intimately without having to write directly about yourself." The pact makes saying no harder but makes saying yes so much more satisfactory, so much more humane.

University of Chicago is a four-year private university and liberal arts college for men and women, located in Chicago, Illinois.

WESLEYAN UNIVERSITY

> **"Can the college application essay make a difference in our child's chances of acceptance?"**

Karl M. Furstenberg
Dean of Admission and Financial Aid

Students' ability to express themselves in writing is crucial to their success in college. The college application essay, a specific example of writing, can give a clear picture of a student's capabilities. The essay might support or refute other information in the student's application file, such as grades, activities, teachers' comments, or standardized test scores. Often, all of the application "evidence" about a student, including the essay, is consistent. Then the essay simply adds color to the image or confirms abilities or attributes that were already apparent in the remainder of the student's application file.

But a college application essay can make a real difference when information in a student's application appears contradictory. Imagine the following situation. Applicant Julie comes highly recommended by her high school counselor and math teacher. They describe her as diligent and conscientious, though her French teacher notes that "she could do better." Julie's SAT scores are superior. Her Achievement Test scores are weaker. Most of Julie's grades are excellent, although there are occasional marks below her high standards. An additional reference mentions Julie's tendency to become bored easily.

Such a mixture of information leaves the admission officer in a quandary. The lower Achievement Tests compared to the aptitude test might suggest that Julie isn't well motivated. But those results instead could be due to a less than rigorous high school program. Perhaps that is all her school offers. Or is that all Julie chose to take? Two teachers find her hardworking. One feels she could do more. Why? Maybe Julie lacks discipline. Or perhaps Julie has few intellectual peers and is frustrated by superficial conversations and activities.

Information in Julie's application file raises some questions about her motivation and commitment. Her application essay could help to answer those questions. Imagine the conclusion the admission committee would reach if Julie submitted an essay that was disjointed and dashed off at the last minute. Imagine the difference in the committee's impression if Julie's essay were a thoughtful, carefully crafted piece discussing her desire for a greater challenge.

The topic of a college application essay can be valuable as a reflection of a student's personal interests and qualities, though the topic itself doesn't necessarily need to convey these messages. It is how a student treats a topic and what he or she invests in it that can create a successful statement.

Selective colleges in particular have the advantage of choosing from a large number of applicants to form a community of people who will grow and learn from each other. Personal qualities such as originality, sincerity, and curiosity can be highlighted in an application essay. The essay can indicate how a student thinks, what is meaningful to him or her, and what the applicant sees as his or her own strengths. Actually, the application essay is more a "thinking sample" than a writing sample, and the student should view it as an opportunity to present himself or herself. By means of a very good essay, a student can emerge as a person rather than as a collection of data. Admission officers are more likely to be advocates of people than statistics. A truly successful essay will provoke some sort of response in the reader.

As a final note, students should use common sense in writing their college application essays because good judgment is respected. Conversely, inappropriate themes can hurt. Yes, risk taking is esteemed, but honesty is the best policy. A college application is not enhanced by the use of gimmicks that are unrelated to who a student really is as a person.

The best advice a student can follow is this: Think. Exert reasonable effort. Write. Wait a couple of weeks. Reread. If you're satisfied with the essay and you think it is a candid reflection of your personality as well as a good indication of your ability and style, submit it. Don't overedit it—you'll lose the spark of spontaneity. Don't seek the advice of too many others—you'll lose your own voice. And above all, don't ask anyone else to write it for you. Admission committees expect the essay to be *your* work, not someone else's. Essay writing can be an educational and pleasurable experience for you—a chance to make an honest statement that makes a difference. Good luck!

Wesleyan University is a four-year private university and liberal arts college for men and women, located in Middletown, Connecticut.

STANFORD UNIVERSITY

> "We heard about a kid who got into
> Yale with an essay about socks lost in
> the dryer! Will only a high-risk essay
> get our teen into a highly selective
> school?"

John Bunnell
Associate Dean of Admission

There are many stories current among high school students and their parents about weird essays that "got someone in" to this college or that university. Of all the elements of the application, it seems the essay attracts these stories most. But the essay is only one of the elements that students are judged by. And no more than someone can say a teacher's recommendation "got me in," or a certain SAT score made all the difference, at Stanford the essay cannot "get you in."

Essays, of course, are important to us. We get some high-risk essays, some very poor essays, and a lot of good solid reasonable pieces of writing. Some applicants do interesting and unusual things with our questions and the results can be very effective. However, if a student isn't a high-risk taker to begin with, hasn't taken honors and advanced placement courses and made a special contribution in an unusual way, then a high-risk essay just doesn't fit with the rest of the application.

For example, a student discusses a preliminary interest in writing and English. We expect the folder to reveal strong SAT verbal and English Achievement Test scores, a first-rate recommendation from an English teacher, challenging courses in the language arts, and—as a part of this pattern—a substantial, perhaps even a creative, essay. Our admission process allows for quite a bit of value judgment about a student's high school program. We expect to see a coherence among the different parts of the application; the essay must fit with the program, the scores, and the rest of the credentials.

Each year, we look at our essay questions and ask ourselves what we have learned from this batch, what the responses have revealed about students' academic credentials, their drive, motivation, ability to think, and ability to write. We discuss how our applicants' responses helped us judge their fit with Stanford. But the eccentric responses do not automatically correlate with acceptances. There are essays every year that admission counselors post on their bulletin boards to share with colleagues: "Wait till you hear this one!" There are essays on "the joy of sets" or "I am a nerd" that we never forget. Some of these authors are accepted and some are not. Although some essays become famous in the office, others become infamous. There is a fine line between effective humor and embarrassing goofiness or off-putting flippancy. Asked for the one word that best describes oneself, one applicant wrote "concise"—a response neither witty nor revealing to the reader. The state swimmer who used "wet" had a better idea.

It is the total package that helps us make the decision. Perhaps the problem is that some students who are accepted perceive their acceptance in a different way than we have. And once here, they tell the story: "It was my essay on lost socks that got me in." But this is never the case.

Our advice about the application essay is "Be yourself." It is painfully obvious when a student writes to fit his or her cooked-up vision of what a Stanford freshman should be and say. We want the essay tailored to us, written for our question, and confined to the length limits we give. That's part of the exercise, and not reading the instructions is a good way to self-destruct. Those applicants who dare to do this probably produce the "high-risk" essays that have the most positive impact.

Stanford University is a four-year private university for men and women, located in Stanford, California.

Ten Common Essay Topics
Colleges Pose

No matter how many bribes you may offer up to your favorite god of college admission, your college-bound offspring will probably have to write one or more application essays. To give you an idea of what your teenager can expect, here's a list of essay topics that ten selective colleges have recently posed on their college applications, along with some advice for your teen on how to tackle them.

Hamilton College

"Write about a special interest, experience, achievement, or anything else you would like us to know about you."

Take this open-ended chance and run with it. If necessary, use the essay to give more information about a particular aspect of your application.

Boston University

"If you had an opportunity to interview any prominent person—living, deceased, or fictional—whom would you choose and why?"

Remember, choice is important here. It says something about you. Don't pick Lisa Bonet or Sean Penn.

Georgetown University

"Please tell us your thoughts about your future. How do these thoughts relate to your choice of major?"

Talk about specific career possibilities and motivations. Don't talk about money.

Northwestern University

"Describe a change you have noticed in yourself or your surroundings."

This topic takes thought and self-observation. A journal from English class might yield some possibilities.

Trinity College (Connecticut)

"What do you think has been the most important social or political movement of the twentieth century? Do you share a personal identification with this cause?"

Make sure you get your facts straight before tackling this one!

Dartmouth College

"Discuss the greatest challenge you have had to face or expect to face."

Be specific here, rather than far-reaching, idealistic, or quirky.

Simmons College

"How do you think attending Simmons will affect your future?"

Talk about how the school will contribute to your personal growth as well as prepare you for a career. Location, program, and style of teaching may relate here.

Pace University

"Attach an autobiographical account."

This is not a life history. Make it a focused story that will capture the reader's interest. ▶

Bryn Mawr College

"What have you read that has had a specific significance to you? Explain."

This essay can be very personal. Use a short quotation or two from the book to demonstrate what you are talking about. And choose a book you liked, not one you think is impressive.

Bucknell University

"Evaluate a significant experience or achievement that has special meaning for you."

Be particular about the "meaning." The experience should have done more than just "made you a better person."

Making the Most of
Interviews, Campus Visits,
and Outside Help

" 'You should say what you mean,' the March Hare
went on. 'I do,' Alice hastily replied, 'at least I mean
what I say—that's the same thing you know.' "

—LEWIS CARROLL

Now you're in the thick of things. Your teenager is definitely college
bound *somewhere*, but exactly where is another story. At least by now,
your son or daughter should have narrowed the potential college list
to a few genuine choices. It's time to pack the bags and load up the
family car with younger brothers and sisters, guidebooks and maps,
and Mr. or Ms. College Bound to drive to the schools for a first look.

Before you put the key in the ignition, take a moment to read
what the admission professionals in this chapter have to say about
campus visits and interviews. Neither is the high-pressured, grueling
test you and your child might think or have been told, and with a
little "self-psyching," you all can visit colleges and attend admission

interviews with a relaxed, positive attitude. Follow the advice of Herbert Dalton at Middlebury and Beverly Morse at Kenyon: Look at the campus visit as a way to help your teen discover where he or she will feel comfortable spending the next four years, and regard the college interview as the chance for your child to find out what he or she wants to know about college life.

Contrary to some popular opinions, interviews are not the most important part of the admission process, and admission directors are the first to say so. Many schools no longer grant or require interviews. Others rely on alumni or student interns to add a little information and answer applicants' questions. The old adage "To thine own self be true" is the best advice we and the admission professionals can give. It will help your teen live through the interview and successfully get through the rest of life's hurdles that require knowing something about oneself and what one wants. Teach your teen to take control.

Ideally a visit to a college campus, including an interview with an admission representative, should take two days, if you can afford the time and the expense involved. By phone or mail, your teen should schedule an afternoon tour and interview. Then consider the following itinerary:

- Arriving the afternoon before, take a "windshield survey" of the town and campus with your teenager first, and eat dinner in a local restaurant.
- The next day, separate from your teen while he or she attends morning classes and talks to students and professors.
- Meet your teenager for lunch at one of the campus dining halls. Spend time listening to his or her positive and negative impressions, and try to get a sense of campus life.
- If your child likes the school and you don't, or vice versa, give your son or daughter the space to talk. Keep opposite viewpoints to yourself until you and your teen put some physical and emotional distance between yourselves and the place.
- Take your scheduled tour of the campus with your teen and ask plenty of questions of the student tour guide.
- Give your teen a pep talk to prepare for the afternoon interview: "Be polite, be positive, and be proud." No one

likes a wise guy, no one feels comfortable around a whiner or complainer, and no one thinks highly of a person who insists on selling himself or herself short.

If it's inconvenient to make arrangements similar to these, be aware that students can schedule an overnight stay in the dorms of some colleges. Also, colleges sometimes offer "prospective students' days," which give parents and teens an opportunity to get a full dose of classes, programs, and offerings.

If you and your teen are having continual disagreements about college selection, and if his or her guidance counselor is unable to provide all the time and assistance you need, consider hiring some outside counseling. Investigate independent college counselors and be sure of their backgrounds before you engage their services. Edward Wall and Joan Davis, the two experienced professional independents in this chapter, explain how they work, and the credentials box that follows their advice will help you get started.

Whatever you do, don't approach this stage of the college selection process by pushing your parental weight around. Consider the impact of your involvement on your child's self-esteem. One father introduced himself and his son to the admission interviewer by saying, "I give buildings." This didn't get the boy admitted—and it certainly didn't help the father's relationship with his son. Ultimately it is your child's abilities and self-image that will lead to his or her acceptance and success at an institution.

KENYON COLLEGE

> ## "How can our daughter prepare for the college interview? She's very shy and needs some coaching."

M. Beverly Morse
Associate Director of Admission

The college interview is a two-way exchange of educational and personal information that benefits both the student and the college. Although interviews with admission counselors or alumni are not required at many colleges, a student should determine the necessity and the role of the interview at each college long before the application is due.

Each time I interview an anxiety-ridden prospect whose fingers are numb and whose handshake is limp, I want to tell a joke or put the student through a relaxation exercise. Interviews are not the grand inquisition that so many students expect. I would guess that feedback from interviews alters admission decisions in only 5 percent of all cases.

This does not mean that college interviews are unimportant. The prime benefactor is the student, who can get a better feel for a college through the campus visit and interview. Students can ask questions of someone trained to know the facts, provide insight, and offer counseling. The interview is an opportunity for students to talk about themselves and for admission professionals to understand students' educational and personal backgrounds and goals. It can allow students to explain inconsistent scores or grades, to mention an unusual experience, or to elaborate on an exceptional achievement. Through the interview, students can gain a real advocate on the application review staff.

What is exciting for us in admission is that a student can make a fresh impression at a college interview. The interviewed student adds a face and a personality to an application. We like students who show interest in our school, and we are often amazed by what seventeen-year-olds have done.

Preparation makes the college visit and interview more productive. Thorough preparation should include examining personal needs, reading about the college, coming up with insightful questions, making an appointment, and finally arriving at the college with a good attitude, a healthy self-image, and some idea of what to expect.

As parents, you can help your child sort through the mound of college brochures, read college view books, and study guidebooks (both the objective and the entertainingly subjective ones). You can then encourage your child to look beyond cost at this initial stage and ask in person about financial aid. You can foster a positive self-image, which may have been unnecessarily deflated by learning about the average SAT or ACT scores at some ideal colleges. Remind your child that *average* does not mean "minimum"! Also, it is okay to have a long list of questions for an interviewer, but it is not absolutely necessary. One secondary school counseling office prints a list of "One Hundred Tough Questions for Your College Interviewer." We have heard them all and think that those questions only make the student appear less than original.

Because many of the more popular—but not necessarily more selective—colleges get booked up early, students should make interview appointments with the college admission receptionist at least two weeks in advance. It is unnecessary and undesirable to talk directly with the admission director to make this arrangement. If Veterans' Day is the only day your child is free (along with most other high school seniors), I would advise six months' advance notice! Let your child set up the appointment and research travel arrangements. I remember overhearing a conversation between our receptionist and a parent who was demanding an interview on Thanksgiving Day because the child had the day off. The father finally hung up after insisting that if we were at all interested in his child, we would accommodate his needs. Admission counselors are human, too—our employers give us some of the major holidays off, even though we work on Saturday mornings part of the year in addition to five days a week.

It also seems popular to demand that the interview be with the college's director or dean of admission. All interviewers are trained professionals whose input carries the same weight as the director's. The main difference is that during the interview the director may be preoccupied with an upcoming meeting with the college president or with a sticky computer problem. Many colleges will provide visitors' guides that suggest the best and the worst times to visit. These guides were developed for a purpose: to help you and your child have a meaningful visit. Also, remember that attending the interview is not the only reason for a college visit.

You and your child should allow enough time for the college visit and for getting to and from the campus. Don't be like one student who arrived from the Cleveland airport ten minutes before the interview and then declined to take a campus tour afterward because he had to catch the next limo back. In your planning, allow time for a forty-five-minute interview, questions, a campus tour, a class or two, and a chat with students, faculty, and athletic coaches. Help your child avoid being a drop-in who runs the risk of no interview or a no-show who could not be bothered to cancel an appointment. Some colleges will no longer let no-shows reschedule appointments.

Once on campus, your child makes an impression the minute he or she walks into our admission office. We may make more than a mental note when the student oversleeps, shows up more than an hour late, looks a mess, and then gets angry when we are no longer available. Make sure your child dresses comfortably and is awake enough to interview well. Your child is applying to a college, not a law firm. I do not recommend a three-piece suit on a humid, ninety-degree day. On the other hand, I also remember the day one student arrived after hitchhiking from Los Angeles via Stanford, Reed, Carleton, and the University of Chicago and before heading off to Swarthmore, Princeton, Yale, Wesleyan, and Harvard. The student's physical presence made it obvious on that hot summer day that he had been in transit and had not seen a shower in days. Fortunately he was prepared, enthusiastic, and articulate; I quickly got beyond my first impression.

Students make impressions in other ways. Take, for example, the student who wrote her application essay on a biking trip she took through Europe one summer and the joy of the independence, growth, and responsibility she experienced. Yet this same student, who lived only thirty-five miles from the college, indicated on the application that she could not come for an interview!

Students should be themselves at the interview and should let us know and address their needs. If this is a student's first interview, we will understand his or her nervousness. After all, we have all gone through the college admission process. We want to hear your child describe any special academic, housing, and dining needs. We would also rather hear about a sticky situation directly from the student than from the college counselor, principal, or headmaster.

Because competition can be stiff, your child will want to distinguish himself or herself. For example, students who name-drop should be prepared to discuss the authors, scientists, or artists they mention in greater detail. Having some knowledge of the institution shows that there is some real interest in it. Students should get beyond the "What is your student-to-faculty-ratio?" questions—which are answered in the view book—and talk about the details that determine whether or not the college is a good match for the student. These details might include academic advising, educational philosophy, opportunities to continue important extracurriculars, career counseling, or graduate school placement.

By the way, don't be offended when we invite your child into the interview room and leave you behind for a half hour. This is your child's college interview, not yours. You will, of course, have your chance to ask questions at the conclusion of the interview.

If you and your child are unable to make it to a college campus for a visit and an interview, you may be able to meet with one of the alumni of the college in your area. Many colleges have a network of alumni who interview candidates locally. These alumni are given updates annually on factual information, and most know not to drift into a blissful monologue about their student days. Instead, they are trained to provide the admission office with insightful reports based on their interviews with students. Yes, the alumni interview counts the same as an on-campus interview. The main difference is that the student does not get to see the school, meet students and faculty, or experience the campus community.

Whether off campus or on, interviews best suit everyone's needs when they take place between May of the student's junior year and the application deadline in the senior year. Your child may find out that a particular college does not suit his or her academic or social needs and save everyone the cost and labor of the application. Do not allow the interview to be postponed until your child is placed on a waiting list.

No two interviews, of course, are exactly alike, but some are more memorable than others. I'll never forget Rachel. Trying to impress me with her love of opera and theater, she leaped up from her chair and serenaded me and my entire office with an aria from *Aida*. I'll also remember David. After describing his expertise in riflery, he flung himself on the floor to show me the correct position for shooting. Then there was Edward. Although he said almost nothing at his interview, two years later his nail marks can still be seen in the armrests of my chair. And finally Rita. A firm believer in the occult, Rita assured me that her ouija board had advised her to leave Albuquerque and come to Ohio to follow her destiny as either a student or a dishwasher at a local restaurant!

The college interview is not a grilling. Relax, remember that there are no "correct" responses to interview questions, and allow us to help the whole family through the admission process. Learn what you can. An interview alone is *not* the basis of an admission decision.

Kenyon College is a four-year private liberal arts college for men and women, located in Gambier, Ohio.

MIDDLEBURY COLLEGE

"Some colleges offer visits to the campus. Would such a visit help our child get accepted?"

Herbert F. Dalton, Jr.
Director of Enrollment Planning

The key to a successful college campus visit is what you and your child do before the visit actually takes place. This means researching colleges and getting your list of schools down to a manageable number. Any more than eight college visits is excessive. Visiting too many can be overwhelming; one college begins to blend into another, and it becomes difficult for your child to get the essence of any one place.

The visit—and indeed the entire college admission process— should be a natural extension of your family relationship. If you and your child ordinarily do things together, it makes sense to visit colleges together. If you don't, accompanying your child may well be counterproductive.

When should applicants and their families visit the schools on their list? Unfortunately, there's no ideal time. Most students visit colleges after their junior year, during the summer or fall. Both times have disadvantages as well as advantages. Prospective students have more time in the summer than they do in the fall, but many campuses don't have their regular student population in the summer. The fall has the advantage of presenting the campus as it really is but the disadvantage of bad timing for the candidate. Most high school seniors can ill afford to miss classes in the fall, their most crucial academic semester. My advice is to visit all colleges on the pared-down list in the summer and then, if need be, return to the top one or two campuses in the fall for short visits.

What should your child do when he or she visits a college campus? First, your child should schedule enough time to see the school. At least three hours should be allowed for a tour, an interview, and some informal browsing. You and your child can also schedule a meeting with the person on campus who oversees your child's special area of interest, whether it be the swimming coach or an astronomy professor.

The tour. Ideally the campus tour should be scheduled before the college interview. This is the chance for you and your child to get a feel for the college. What does the campus look like? What are the students and faculty like? Don't judge the college by the tour guide; he or she is only one member of the student body and may not be representative. Chances are the tour guide is a good spokesperson, though, and knows the answers to many of your questions. Ask questions, but be careful not to dominate the conversation. Listen to the questions your child asks.

The interview. First, make sure your child knows the difference between the two types of college interviews and knows which type has been scheduled. The "group interview" is a misnomer; it's actually a group information session. Usually a member of the admission office staff presents a brief overview of the college and then answers questions; most often parents are invited to participate with their child.

A personal interview is a one-on-one encounter between your child and a member of the college admission staff, sometimes a student, but more often a decision maker on the admission staff. The personal interview generally lasts about forty-five minutes and, at its best, is a *conversation*. In most cases, parents have a chance to meet the interviewer, too. Again, the "don't dominate" rule applies. Too many good interviews come undone when a parent tries to impress and impose. If you do participate at the end of the interview, avoid asking questions your child may have already asked.

To schedule an interview, your child should call—not write to— the college admission office well in advance. Several weeks is usually adequate but in some cases may not be enough. Colleges have a finite number of appointments available for personal interviews, and it is a matter of first come, first served. Group sessions, on the other hand, can be scheduled at the last minute and often require no advance notice. To make maximum use of the time on campus, you and your child should know the schedule of such sessions and tours before visiting.

Even though you'll want to take a back seat during the campus visit, there are things you can do to help your child have a productive, comfortable interview. Here are a few tips to share with your child:

- ☐ Arrive on time.
- ☐ Be prepared. Know the basic facts about the college, the sort of information that is included in any view book. A student doesn't have to memorize the catalog, but he or she should know the institution's size, types of academic programs, and the like.
- ☐ Converse. Be prepared to ask questions and to listen. If you want some indication of the types of questions you may be asked, look at the application. The colleges that ask way-out essay questions on their application forms have a tendency to do likewise in their interviews.
- ☐ The one question the interviewee will always be asked is "Do you have any questions?" Asking questions conveys that the student is prepared and interested in the college.
- ☐ Avoid excuses. The interview should not be wasted in a long explanation of a deficient record or low test scores.
- ☐ Have fun.

Both you and your child should remember that the personal interview is more informational than evaluative. The college will be trying to sell itself as much as your child is trying to sell himself or herself. So relax. If your child isn't qualified, he or she won't interview his or her way in. A good interview—one in which the candidate demonstrates love of life, love of learning, and other intangibles— can have an impact on a student's candidacy at some colleges. Generally it is more important at a private institution than at a public one, and the smaller the college, the greater its impact.

Don't forget to write down the interviewer's name. This person is your child's human contact with the college and its admission operation. If you have questions to ask or new information to convey at midyear, your child can call the interviewer. If the interview goes well and your child likes the college, it is appropriate to write the interviewer a thank-you note. At the very least, this ensures that someone in the admission office will remember your child!

Browsing time. As you and your child wander around the campus and its buildings, be sure to look at bulletin boards; they will tell you how students spend their time. What is the campus culture? Is it politically active? Is it culturally dead? Is everyone looking for a ride home on weekends? Visit the snack bar. Are there lots of cliques? Do students sit with professors? Observe facial expressions and gaits—they can tell you about the campus mood.

Finally, a word about the ride home. In the campus visit, as in the rest of the college admission process, parents can be especially helpful as a sounding board. Being there to listen on the ride home from the campus, or when your child returns from a solo trip, can provide invaluable support.

Middlebury College is a four-year private liberal arts college for men and women, located in Middlebury, Vermont.

INDEPENDENT COLLEGE COUNSELOR

> ## "What is an independent college counselor?"

Edward B. Wall
Gibbs and Wall Educational Consultants
Amherst, Massachusetts

Why do independent college counselors exist? The answer is that there is a constant, ongoing need for them. They exist because most high school counselors are overworked and underpaid, carry incredibly heavy loads of students, and need all they help they can get. But no matter how large or how small the individual counselor's load, it is impossible to give each student equal time. I know that because, in addition to being an independent counselor in the evenings, on weekends, during school vacations, and all summer long, I am also an institutional counselor responsible for a senior class of 130 college-bound youngsters—70 directly—and a junior class of 100, with one full-time and one part-time counselor assisting me.

At the school where I work, one-quarter to one-third of the students are in attendance because an independent counselor referred them. The independent counselors often are retained by the parents of these students to help with the college admission process. Frankly, I am delighted to have their assistance because I think that two counselors working as advocates for a student are better than one.

Independent counselors also exist because some college admission counselors don't level with prospective candidates about their chances of admission. Why? They are afraid that they might hurt the candidates' feelings. They are afraid that they might lose an applicant in their admission pool. And their hands are all too often tied by faculty members on their admission committees who are caught up in grades and test scores only and won't let admission officers be the counselors and professionals they are or should be. Admission officers should have the courage to discuss with a student his or her realistic chances of being admitted. A detour early in the senior year is preferable to an unexpected knockout blow in April when the candidate is expecting a positive outcome.

Some independent college counselors charge $1000 or more per client. Some charge a good deal less. Whatever they charge, it is considerably less than a down payment on a car, and we all know that these days the cost of a decent car is close to the cost of a year's room, board, tuition, and fees at a private college or university.

Regardless of the charge for their services, what independent college counselors do for their clients varies from counselor to counselor. The first thing I do is to sit down with the student and his or her family for a group discussion about their expectations. Then I comment candidly on those expectations based on information obtained from the student's transcript, including courses, grades, and test scores.

What follows next is an in-depth interview with the student alone. We take a critical look at his or her list of potential colleges, adding to and deleting from that list, which may swell to as many as thirty-five or forty colleges, depending on the client's credentials. Developing this list is most important because to many students the names of some excellent options are unfamiliar: Pomona might as well be Xanadu. I expect the client to visit at least ten to fifteen colleges during the summer. Then the list is boiled down to eight to twelve by September 1 and six to eight by Thanksgiving if the student is a regular applicant.

I recommend applying to four groups of colleges in a descending order of competition: (1) the "longshot"—one, two, or three chances in ten of being admitted, (2) the "fifty-fifty"—one in two odds, (3) the "likely"—about seven in ten odds, and (4) the "safety"—a ten-in-ten chance of being admitted. I usually urge six applications: one "longshot," two "fifty-fifties," two "likelies," and one "safety." I am candid when a client mentions a college I think is unlikely, and I also suggest that he or she seriously consider taking a year off between high school and college when I think that option is an appropriate one.

I don't make appointments for personal interviews for my clients, and I frown on independent counselors who do. That responsibility rests with the clients and their families. If I did this work for them, I would not be helping them in the long run. Usually, the in-depth session that I have with clients is the only face-to-face interaction, mainly because most come from great distances. However, I do exchange a great deal of correspondence and have many long-distance telephone calls with clients.

Only in an emergency—a late-spring client who is on six waiting lists or a new client in April who has been shot down everywhere—do I ever telephone a college admission office. I never try to shoehorn a student into a selective college by harassing admission deans. One reason I refuse to telephone a college except in an emergency is that I remember how much I resented calls from independent counselors when I was a college admission officer!

Nor do I help students with their college essays, perhaps the most overblown aspect of the entire process, unless it is to suggest a topic. I had to laugh recently when I read an article in which an independent counselor was quoted as saying, "And this was the thirteenth session I had with that client on the essay!" Whose essay was it in the end?

The letter of recommendation is my most important contribution to the client's admission file. Many college admission officers say that they don't want letters of recommendation from independent counselors. If I did not write a letter of recommendation to my former admission colleagues, with most of whom I have relationships of trust, I would feel that I was not doing my job.

Independent counselors can provide the proper professional guidance and support that students and their parents need during the college selection process. With an independent counselor's help, a student may be less likely to wake up in the dorm early one December morning—having flunked the biology midterm the day before—and wonder, "What am I doing here?"

Edward Wall is a partner in Gibbs and Wall, college and independent school counselors, with offices in Allentown, Pennsylvania; Byfield, Massachusetts; and Brunswick, Maine.

JOAN DORMAN DAVIS
COLLEGE ADMISSION
❦ C O U N S E L O R ❦

INDEPENDENT COLLEGE COUNSELOR

> ## "We're thinking about hiring an independent college counselor for our child. Are they worth the cost?"

Joan Dorman Davis
College Admission Counselor
Seattle, Washington

I'll never forget a testy conference I had with a boy from an eastern Washington town of fifteen hundred people. He'd brought his college applications and rough drafts of his application essays into my counseling office. I read through his laborious essay on "Why I hope to go to Brown" and shook my head.

"Do you really want to be admitted to Brown?" I asked him. "Yes, I do," he replied. "Then you've got to write a new essay," I told him. He looked annoyed. I waited. "What's wrong with this one?" he asked. I replied, "Any kid from anywhere could have written it. It doesn't give a clue about *your* background, what makes you tick."

We talked about what makes an effective application essay. We brainstormed some ideas. He went home, started over, and wrote about installing a sprinkler system in his parents' two-acre front yard. He gave the Brown University admission people something they could

171

work with, a glimpse of a kid in action. Brown admitted him; he went.

This student learned what to do to give Brown his best shot. And from the experience of rewriting, he learned about himself, his resilience, and his writing skills. *He* chose to try again, and it paid off.

Another boy I counseled wrote me a letter about his successful freshman year at Trinity College in Connecticut. He closed his letter with this statement: "I'm glad you told me about Trinity. I'd never heard of it, so I never would have applied." Many families I work with are unaware of their children's college options. As a matchmaker of kids and colleges, I enlarge a student's focus beyond familiar local universities. Families tend to be receptive to my help, saying, "We want our child to be happy, to have a good experience at college." Families trust my recommendations and act on them, confident that they are on the right track.

Finally, there's Jean, the star volleyball, basketball, and softball player at her high school. I first met all five-feet-eleven of her during her sophomore year. Her transcript showed straight A's in an uninspired course load. I talked with her about beefing it up. "How about taking advanced mathematics in summer school, an extra two years of Spanish, and advanced placement English?" Stubbornly independent, Jean would have preferred to make all her decisions on her own, but she dreamed of an athletic scholarship to Stanford University. She took my advice.

For the next two years, Jean endured cracks from her classmates about "being a brain" and such remarks from her teachers as "Why do you think you need to take calculus? Plenty of other kids from our school have gone to college without it." She earned top grades in a back-breaking course load, picking up courses at the local community college to fill in the gaps. We'll never know if Jean could have been accepted at Stanford because she never applied. Instead, she enrolled at Colorado College, where the coaches assured her of their support for her as a scholar and an athlete in two sports.

Jean's story illustrates two points. First, an independent college counselor can show students why a rigorous academic program counts. Second, an independent college counselor can tutor kids to ask probing questions that will deflect the dazzle of a famous college name. As she explored a variety of top colleges, Jean concluded that at a smaller college she was more likely to succeed as a scholar and an athlete. She entered Colorado College confident that she was prepared to handle both the academics and the athletics.

Is an independent college counselor worth the cost? Of course, some high schools provide the kind of in-depth, organized, thoughtful counseling that students need, but it's hit or miss. Many public school counselors' job descriptions barely mention college counseling. In Seattle, public school counselors typically oversee four hundred students each year. College counseling is a low priority; drug counseling, discipline, and course registration come first. "I'm not an expert on colleges," said one public school counselor. "I'm glad to refer families to an independent if they want the detailed, in-depth services that you offer."

Even at pricey private high schools, college counseling may lack luster. One student told me, "It seemed that the counselor at my school recommended the same six colleges to half the senior class. For most of the kids, those colleges were fine. For me, they weren't. Instead of helping me, he ignored me."

Sometimes students in the bottom half of a high school class are slighted. I've heard these students comment: "I'm not outstanding, so I'm overlooked," and "Just because I had a weak freshman year, the college counselor thinks that I'm not qualified to apply to private colleges."

Or students and parents may want a second opinion. "Call it insurance, but our daughter's college education is something we've saved for. Applying to the right college is complicated. We want the best information available as we make decisions," said the parents of one of my clients.

Applying to college is an increasingly complex, competitive undertaking. Independent college counselors are interpreters of trends, procedures, and college literature; we are experts on college life, curricula, and standards at scores of colleges. We hustle, visiting dozens of campuses annually, never missing an opportunity to quiz an admission dean, and we participate in myriad professional meetings, workshops, and college fairs. We're skeptics—we don't believe everything we hear; we prefer to draw our own conclusions about colleges from a wide assortment of sources. Experienced professionals, many of us have worked in college admission offices or high school guidance offices, and our fees range from $125 to $1,200, depending on the extent of services that families choose. Some independent counselors even take on a number of scholarship clients and waive fees when need merits it.

Do the families I work with value my services? Yes. More than a quarter of my clients each year are the siblings of former clients. I rarely advertise; 95 percent of my clients are referred to me by former clients.

Here's how I measure my success: If a student has applied to appropriate colleges, has been admitted to at least one college that he or she will attend with enthusiasm, I've done a good job of matchmaking. If the student has learned from the process something about himself or herself, about decision making, and about the world beyond the walls of high school, I've done a good job of counseling.

Every student who has completed my counseling program has been admitted to college. I can count on one hand the number of clients who have left college after freshman year, compared to the national average of more than 45 percent who don't persist. As an independent college counselor, I don't "get them in"—students do it themselves. But I *do* provide specific, timely guidance at a critical period, when students are receptive to it.

Independent college counselors make a difference. For families who care about expanding their college options, making informed decisions about college, and making a match that works, our services are worth considering.

Joan Dorman Davis is an independent college admission counselor in Seattle, Washington, and publisher of College Bound, *a monthly newsletter on college selection and admission.*

Credentials for Independent College Consultants

If you think that you and your child might benefit from some outside help after initial meetings with the school counselor and the first weeks of college searching, make sure the independent consultant you choose for the job meets these qualifications:

□ **The Right Experience.** Be sure the independent consultant you are interested in hiring has experience in the field. The consultant may have worked previously as an admission counselor at a college or as a guidance counselor at a high school. Find out where the person worked and for how long. Important credentials in the field are membership in the National Association of College Admission Counselors (NACAC) and in the Independent Educational Consultants Association (IECA), which both require professional experience for acceptance. Avoid consultants who use their own children's experience as the basis of their expertise. If you wish, check out the consultant with a local college.

□ **The Right Price.** Prices for independent consulting vary widely, depending on the geographic area, the independent consultant, and, if the consultant has one, the size of his or her consulting firm. Make sure you can afford the price on top of other impending college expenses.

□ **The Right Service.** Ask for a detailed list of the services you and your child will receive for the price you are asked to pay. Ask what part you and your child will play in helping the independent consultant provide those services and how much time the consultant will spend advising your child. Do not be fooled by a battery of personality or preference tests. These should not be the basis for hefty fees. And be wary of help that is too invasive. Your child's applications and essays must ultimately be his or her own.

❏ **The Right Referrals.** Talk to other parents and students whom the independent consultant has helped. If you don't know of any, ask the consultant for the names of past clients in your area. Make sure you listen to the parents' *and* the students' evaluations.

Before you seek the help of an independent college consultant, don't forget your child's high school counselor. No matter how you go about it, records, transcripts, and a good portion of your child's application will be handled through the secondary school. If you use an independent consultant, be sure your child's guidance counselor is aware of this, not as a threat but as a supplemental source of information.

According to Nicky Carpenter, a Minnesota independent college consultant and former President of IECA, the credentials we've listed are important qualifications that every independent college consultant needs in order to counsel college-bound students effectively. If you want to engage the help of an independent but don't know of any, she recommends calling the colleges in your area for names.

The Financial Aid Hurdle

"Money is like muck. It does no good unless it's spread around."

—FRANCIS BACON

If you think the cost of living has gone up, take a look at the cost of learning! The costs at a private college, and even those at a large state school, can be sobering. They can range from a low of about $15,000 to a high of about $70,000. And that's just for four years. With graduate school a popular option these days, the sooner you as parents begin planning for college costs, the better. By comparison, your own education will seem like a bargain. Who would have believed that what cost your parents $12,000 two decades ago would cost you $70,000 today?

Why have college costs risen at such a rate? Like all things, they have been subject to inflation. They have also risen faster than inflation because many college costs have themselves outstripped the inflation rate. Insurance, for example, has risen 17.5 percent. Maintenance, facilities upkeep, printing, and paper are considerably more expensive. And colleges are now expected to provide facilities that we as students did without—gymnasiums must be sports centers; writing workshops need twenty computer terminals. Of course, faculty salaries represent a large part of a college's costs. Many schools are trying to make up for the faculty salary erosion of the 1970s, and many tenured faculty now stay on well past sixty-five. In addition, schools are facing competition with each other for big-name professors. A college may find that to keep a top research professor, it must offer a generous salary, expensive facilities, and a minimal teaching load.

Financial aid is another enormous expense for which colleges must budget. As college costs increase, so do the numbers of students who qualify as needy. Less federal and state money now has to be divided among a larger pool. At the same time, many colleges have increased their commitment of financial aid to needy students and each year try to allocate more money to the financial aid budget. A college that cannot fund all the needy students it would like to accept—and there are many schools in this situation—finds itself between a rock and a hard place.

Robert Jaycox of Colgate University describes how the complex issue of financial aid has changed in the last twenty years. Today financial aid is complicated by forms, requirements, federal and state laws, and a variety of choices and options. Parents need to plan for college costs as soon as possible and to educate themselves early about what the federal government will do, what the state has to offer, and how individual colleges can contribute to the financial aid package. Richard Black of Berkeley explains how the eight campuses in the University of California (UC) system draw on funds from all three sources to meet the needs of admitted students. Like UC, most schools will offer a student a package of aid based on a grant, a loan, and a job, according to the need demonstrated and the family contribution possible. Filling out the Financial Aid Form (FAF) is usually the first step toward getting assistance. Suzanne Schlager of Sarah Lawrence College outlines some of the other steps.

If your child is a high achiever, either in the classroom or on the high school playing fields, he or she may be a candidate for a merit scholarship or an athletic scholarship. Merit scholarships are awards based not on need but on academic achievement or some talent or special qualification. As David Erdmann of Rollins College will tell you, many colleges use merit scholarships to recruit the best and the brightest. They use athletic scholarships for a similar purpose—to attract star players for their sports teams. Scott Healy and Andrew Burgess of Penn State will acquaint you with some of the National Collegiate Athletic Association (NCAA) rules and regulations govern-

178

ing athletic scholarships. If your son or daughter is a likely candidate for one of these scholarships, you'll also want to read the *NCAA Guide for the College-Bound Student Athlete*.

College financial aid advisors often talk about creative financing. Many parents who do not qualify as needy find tuition payments a burden, but there are ways to prepare for these payments. Milosh Mamula of Allegheny College offers some thoughts on keeping out of the poorhouse while still paying for college.

Most financial aid officers agree that parents need to broaden the window on the financial aid question, looking to the college years not as the beginning of a long period of indebtedness but rather as the culmination of the thinking and planning that began in the hospital delivery room. College costs certainly justify a long-term strategy of preparation. Ideally, a knowledge of what's available, how need is calculated, and what loan and payment options exist should be developed as soon as the college-bound newborn starts sleeping through the night.

COLGATE UNIVERSITY

"How has the financial aid picture changed during the last twenty years?"

Robert P. Jaycox
Director of Student Aid

In the last twenty years, the face of financial aid has changed greatly. As always, there is good news and bad news. The good news is that state and federal programs have been broadened to allow substantially increased access to government funds. The bad news is that the process of applying for financial aid has become more complicated, doubling the paperwork for both parents and colleges. The changes within the financial aid field involve four areas: state and federal funding, financing options, new family structures, and increased student attendance.

First, there are differences in how well state and federal programs are funded and how eligibility for these funds is determined. In the 1970s, many people believed that the state and federal governments were going to "do it all." This applied to a variety of programs, and education was certainly one of them. In the 1980s, with deficit reduction a major problem, the government drew the line, making clear that it did not intend to foot the whole bill. Although the cutbacks in student financial aid have not been as severe as the media would have us believe, some marginal and "no-need" categories of loans

180

have been eliminated. In the past, for instance, the needs test for Guaranteed Student Loans (GSLs) was based on income alone; now it is based on assets, too.

Second, there has been a broadening of focus. College financial aid offices have added to their repertoire a variety of financing options. In the late 1960s, it was assumed that parents would bear the burden of their child's education. A year at a private college then cost $3,000. As aid became a more prominent part of college financing, the 1970s saw an eclipse of this attitude. Parents heard about other children receiving aid and came to feel that the government or the college was responsible for funding their child, at least in part. Today, parents are back in the role of primary providers for their child's education, and, naturally, college financial aid officers have responded with guidance, hand holding, and options. Parent education has become a new and challenging part of our work. Financial aid officers now print brochures, go to workshops, and spend hours explaining payment plans, loan options, and "creative financing" to parents. The payment plans and the loan options we now offer are our response to the change in the role of parents and to the escalating costs of a college education.

Third, financial aid has responded to social change. The "non-nuclear" family is more and more the rule, and the complexities of divorced parents, stepparents, and nonmarried heads of households have added to the complications of financial aid, as has the issue of when a student is an "independent." It is now much harder to determine a family's ability to pay, and the increased paperwork and bureaucratic processing have made the job more time-consuming for parents as well as financial aid officers. As many parents are discovering, one can, with sufficient tenacity and money, divorce a spouse, but one cannot divorce a child. The obligations remain even when Dad quits the law firm and cuts loose to do his own thing making pots in Vermont.

Finally, despite the enormous cost of a college education, there are more young people going to college and therefore more needy freshmen. Public financial aid monies have increased in absolute dollars, but few programs have been immune to inflation. Consequently, inflation-adjusted dollars are now significantly fewer in number. In the post-Black Monday economy, many colleges are finding themselves dependent on public funds for a large percentage of their financial aid budget, with inadequate resources of their own.

181

What about the future of financial aid? Certainly, deficit reduction must be addressed; the solutions will significantly affect education in this country. In addition, although the Tax Reform Act of 1986 was supposedly a revenue-neutral act, it created disincentives to saving for college that need to be worked out.

The 1990s should see the beginning of a consensus on the role the federal government should play in support of higher education. Nevertheless, there needs to be a better system of financial aid analysis, one that takes into account the larger picture. Parents often find themselves with a significant cash-flow problem when college is imminent. They see student loans as the easiest immediate solution. As a result, the long-range ability of young people to repay these loans has become an issue. Needs analysis is presently a momentary snapshot of the ability to pay in a particular year. Long-term loans for parents or students and financial packages that include paying some college costs before, some during, and some after college will be more realistic and less burdensome for many parents faced with the high cost of learning.

Like all aspects of the admission process, financial aid is not what it was. In part, the changes are the result of the changing world we find ourselves in; in part, they are the result of the continuing efforts of those in the field to serve the college population—and their parents—more fairly and more fully.

Colgate University is a four-year private liberal arts college for men and women, located in Hamilton, New York.

SARAH LAWRENCE COLLEGE

> **"What kinds of financial aid are available at colleges, and how can our child apply for them?"**

Suzanne Schlager
Director of Financial Aid

As college costs increase, more and more families look for financial assistance in the form of grants, low-interest student loans, and extended payment plans. Here's some important information designed to help you secure the funds necessary to finance your teen's college education today.

To apply for financial aid, make sure you accurately complete the necessary forms and meet important application deadlines. In general, most colleges and universities require you to complete standard, federally approved forms to determine financial need and eligibility for federal, state, and college programs. These forms include the Financial Aid Form (FAF), Family Financial Statement (FFS), and the Federal Student Aid Application. In addition, colleges may require you to complete their institutional forms and, where applicable, the Divorced and Separated Parent Supplement and the Business or Farm Supplement. Deadlines for completing these forms vary among institutions and may be found in college catalogs; however, in all cases, it is important to begin filing the necessary forms for aid at the same time your teenager applies for admission. Waiting until your teenager is accepted by a college may jeopardize his or her chances of receiving institutional funds.

Most of the financial aid available to students from the federal government, state agencies, and institutional programs is based on family financial need. Colleges and universities use a federally approved system to evaluate family income and assets. Their analysis considers your necessary household expenses, as well as the size of your family and the number of family members attending college. After these expenses are deducted, a portion of your remaining family income and assets is assumed to be available to pay for college. This amount, plus a standard contribution from your child's summer earnings and a portion of his or her assets, constitutes your family contribution. The family contribution is then subtracted from the college's total cost of education—including tuition, fees, housing, food, books, personal expenses, and transportation—to determine your financial need.

Because financial aid packages are based not only on your ability to pay but also on the cost of attending a specific institution, you and your teen may very well discover that schools that you thought were too expensive are actually within your range. So don't rule out a favorite choice just because it carries a high price tag.

Consider the case of Linda. Although Linda's parents were convinced they couldn't afford to send her to one of her first-choice colleges, they didn't have the heart to stop her from applying to them, along with some more affordable universities. She applied for financial aid at all of the schools. After being accepted at her first-choice college and one of the more affordables, Linda received a financial aid package from both schools. Her parents were amazed at the amount of money in the form of grants and loans that she was awarded because they didn't understand how the concept of *need* works. What parents can contribute to college costs is a fixed number determined by the FAF. Linda's contribution was not greater at the more expensive school; rather Linda's financial *need* was greater. Therefore, she was awarded a much larger financial aid package there—which actually made the costs of attending the first-choice college about the same as the costs of attending the other school. With the financial aid and a part-time job, Linda was able to attend her first-choice college.

Once your financial need is calculated, the college's financial aid administrator develops an aid package to meet that need. Although not all colleges compute your family contribution in exactly the same way, in general, financial aid packages contain three main elements: federal, state, and college grants (which are outright gifts); federally supported student loan programs; and college work-study plans. Besides these need-based programs, many colleges and universities offer extended payment options and long-term loan programs. These plans help families receiving other types of aid to finance their contributions; they also assist families who, because of income and asset levels, do not qualify for the need-based programs. Most colleges whose aid programs are need based offer about the same package in the form of a job, a loan, and a grant. Schools that also have merit or athletic scholarships may offer an applicant additional aid above need in the form of a grant. In general, you can count on your child's aid package being renewed each year, provided your family circumstances remain stable and your teen satisfactorily meets the academic standards set by the institution.

When you and your teenager apply for financial aid at a college, keep these four things in mind:

- Refer to college catalogs for required forms and deadlines, and submit early.
- Keep copies of all forms you submit and, if possible, use certified mail. Obtain a Social Security number for your teenager.
- If your son is eighteen, remind him that he must register for Selective Service.
- Schedule an appointment with the college financial aid administrator. He or she may serve as your most valuable resource in determining eligibility for the college's various aid programs.

It's important to remember that the fundamental principle behind financial aid is that parents and students have the primary responsibility for financing college. As you select a college that meets your son's or daughter's educational goals, remember that timely and careful investigation of the many sources of aid available to families can be instrumental in achieving those goals.

Sarah Lawrence College is a four-year private liberal arts college for men and women, located in Bronxville, New York.

ALLEGHENY COLLEGE

> ## "Our child doesn't qualify for a need-based scholarship. Can you suggest some 'creative financing' to help pay for college?"

Milosh B. Mamula
Director of Student Aid

Planning the financing for college or university study is much like planning the financing for a major purchase, such as an automobile or a home. In addition to the savings we put aside for the purchase, we often must consider loans or mortgages and plan carefully the monthly payments that come from our earnings. Often the planning requires sacrifices and some hairsplitting decisions.

What many of us face when we plan our major purchase is the question of how to pay for the new financial obligation (car payment, home mortgage, or college bill) out of our current operating budget. The issue is cash flow: the ability to meet all of our weekly, monthly, or annual obligations out of our take-home earnings. With some careful planning and perhaps some creative financing, we can meet those objectives.

Savings. Perhaps the most common financing mechanism is planned savings. Studies have shown that, if parents were to begin a thoughtful savings plan early enough (five to eight years in advance of their child's college experience) they would be able to maintain the plan throughout their child's schooling without major disruption in their cash flow. However, by the time most of us really think seriously about how to pay for our child's or children's schooling, we have lost the threshold of optimum return a long-term savings plan offers. We are then faced with the immediate dilemma of how to pay for the schooling out of our current cash flow. If you are in this predicament, the following suggestions and available plans may help you out.

It is never too late to begin to save. If you know your child is starting college in nine months, begin now by budgeting a portion of your weekly or monthly income toward meeting the first billed expense, and continue to save throughout the course of the school year. If you plan early and know that the budgeted saving is in place, you will be less likely to succumb to the impulse to buy a new TV set or a new car and more likely to defer other major purchases. What is most important is the planned effort that puts your budgeting process in perspective.

Payment Plans. Many institutions provide or recommend commercial firms that offer payment plan options to meet the annual or total costs of college. The incentives to consider these payment plans include early payment, life insurance coverage, reduced comprehensive fees, and guaranteed tuition. If an institution has payment plans or payment options that allow for extended budget planning, it will mention them in its literature. Don't be afraid to ask. Financial aid officers can advise you.

Parents exploring these options may find the installment plan most helpful, since it allows for a planned monthly payment within their budget. The small service fees charged by the carrier or by the institution cover the handling and billing expenses. In some instances, the commercial carrier also offers insurance coverage against catastrophic income loss.

Quite often, the costlier private institutions offer a payment option that permits full payment, *at a small discount,* of the comprehensive fee (tuition, room, and board) for the academic year in advance of the school year. This option can yield a saving for the academic year. Some of the same schools also offer a guaranteed tuition plan based on the first year's tuition costs. If parents are able to pay four years of tuition at the beginning of the schooling experience, they can realize a substantial saving, since tuition costs have been increasing at a rate of 6 percent to 10 percent per annum. It should be pointed out that very few schools offer this plan; however, it is an option that you should explore with the admission office or business office of the institutions your child is considering.

Loans. There are long-term loans available to parents from different lending sources that can be used to ease the pressure on direct cash flow if all other financing options are out of the question. The loan parents most frequently use that is not directly determined by financial need is the Parent Loan for Undergraduate Students/Supplemental Loan for Students (PLUS/SLS). PLUS/SLS is a federal loan program available through most local lenders (banks, savings and loan associations, credit unions) and through nationally organized educational loan corporations. Parents with acceptable credit ratings are eligible to borrow up to $4,000 per child enrolled in a postsecondary institution. The loan carries a variable interest rate (10.27 percent for 1987–88) and has a maximum term of ten years. There is a minimum monthly payment of $50 per month, depending upon the amount borrowed. Therefore, a parent borrowing $4,000 for the first time would pay approximately $55 per month while the student is in school, or a total of $660 per year. This would compare to the $400 per month the family would have to pay if it were on a ten-month budget plan, paying the same $4,000 amount. The comparison of $55 per month in loan repayment to $400 per month in a budget plan may be an important consideration in managing your monthly budget or cash flow.

In addition to the PLUS/SLS, many banks, usually larger ones within the community or state, offer sizable educational loans to cover the four years of an undergraduate program. These banks establish a line of credit that parents can draw on to meet educational expenses. Loan amounts can approach $50,000 or $60,000. The loan programs vary with the lender, the amount of the loan, and the credit rating of the borrower. The college or university your child is interested in may have information about lenders that service this type of loan program. Again, ask.

One state loan guaranty agency, the Pennsylvania Higher Education Assistance Agency (PHEAA), provides an alternative loan program for students. Eligibility for a loan in this program is determined by the credit-worthiness of the co-signer of the note, which in most cases is the parent. Pennsylvania residents and non-Pennsylvania residents attending Pennsylvania institutions are eligible to apply for this alternative loan program.

Educational Tuition Plans. Several institutions and state legislatures have modeled educational tuition plans after the one developed by Duquesne University. The Duquesne Alumni Tuition Plan allows an investor (normally a parent) to invest in a child's future college tuition at an early age. The plan assumes a specific investment yield depending upon the age of the prospective student and the intitial year of enrollment. If the child is admitted to the university, the institution will guarantee four years of tuition. However, should the child not be accepted, or choose to attend elsewhere, the initial investment is refunded to the family.

The State of Michigan has enacted a similar program for residents of Michigan, with invested funds applying toward the tuition costs at any institution within the state. The amount of the initial investment is dependent upon the school the investor plans to have his or her child attend. Variations on this tuition plan are being developed by institutions and by several states. These plans are an attempt to reduce the future cost of attending college and are viewed by many as a novel way to plan for the education of our nation's children.

The alternatives in financing college costs are rather extensive. They can be classified into three basic categories: long-term planned savings and investments; planned or enforced budgeting through payment plans; and long-term repayment through loan programs. It is possible to use a combination of any of the above options to achieve the goal of maximizing your cash flow and your ability to meet the varying expenses of your child's college costs.

Allegheny College is a four-year private liberal arts college for men and women, located in Meadville, Pennsylvania.

UNIVERSITY OF CALIFORNIA AT BERKELEY

"How does financial aid work for residents versus out-of-staters?"

Richard Black
Director of Financial Aid

Why did Apple Computer founder Steve Wozniak return to the University of California at Berkeley to complete his undergraduate degree? Perhaps because the educational excellence of this university system is recognized worldwide. We assume that financial support was not an issue for this self-made millionaire. But with a little careful attention to financial aid forms, even the neediest student in California and needy students from anywhere in the nation can afford an education at the University of California.

Parents and students interested in a University of California education should consult college guides to learn the advantages of the eight undergraduate campuses in our system. These guides—*The Public Ivys* by Richard Moll is a good recent one—elaborate on the differences between our two large campuses, Berkeley and Los Angeles (UCLA), and the smaller and newer campuses at Santa Cruz, Riverside, Irvine, Davis, Santa Barbara, and San Diego. For students of superior ability, the university has a major for every interest at one of its campuses.

University of California students who can live at home and commute will find their out-of-pocket expenses to be just a little more than $4,800 in the fall of 1988. About a third of that is for fees, and the rest covers books, transportation, and campus meals. Students who live in the campus residence halls will have costs of about $8,000. In addition to fees, out-of-state students pay tuition, which will probably be $4,500 in the fall of 1988. Their total costs will be about $12,500.

Admission to the University of California is competitive but "need blind." No student is denied admission because of financial need. Best of all, campuses meet full need for almost all admitted students.

Who gets financial aid at Berkeley? Actually 50 percent of the students qualify for scholarships, grants, employment, or loan assistance. Given Berkeley's size and diversity, there is no typical aid recipient, but here are a few representative profiles of past and present (1987–88) recipients:

☐ Francisco is a senior of Hispanic descent from Los Angeles who will study law next year. He has an Affirmative Action grant from Berkeley. In addition, the federal government provides a Pell Grant and a Supplemental Educational Opportunity Grant. Together, these grants provide $3,100 toward his total cost of $7,800. Since his mother can make no contribution toward the cost of his education, he has borrowed $3,100 and earned $1,600 for the remainder of the $7,800 cost of education at Berkeley.

☐ Nancy graduated in 1986 and is now a second-year medical student at a major eastern university. She is of Asian descent and went to a secondary school in the San Francisco Bay Area. As an undergraduate, she was able to qualify for medical school while supporting herself with ten to twelve hours of employment under the Federal College Work-Study Program. Her parents provided about half of her undergraduate costs. The remainder came from an alumni scholarship and a Cal Grant from the California Student Aid Commission.

☐ Joyce hailed from the Midwest, where she participated in A Better Chance, a program for talented black scholars. She too received a Pell Grant, a Minority Scholarship Grant, and employment under the Federal College Work-

191

Study Program. In her work-study job, she was a peer advisor who helped other students secure the aid they needed to complete their education. Joyce was a business major; she recently was offered a position with a prestigious accounting firm.

☐ Peter has received a Drake Scholarship in the Department of Mechanical Engineering. This merit-based award covers the entire cost of his out-of-state fees of $11,806. Peter first learned of this scholarship when he was surveying outstanding mechanical engineering departments as a high school senior and was chosen for the award from a national competition.

As these profiles illustrate, the University of California at Berkeley provides the full complement of federal, state, and institutional scholarships, grants, loans, and employment programs. It is particularly proud of the endowed scholarship program that awards merit scholarships of up to $500 and need-based scholarships of up to $3,000.

The application process to the university is relatively simple, but deadlines are firm because of the more than twenty-five thousand applications processed. Candidates complete the admission application, including the scholarship application, by the end of November and submit the Student Aid Application of California (SAAC) by the required deadline. Out-of-state students are sent an SAAC form by Berkeley. The Financial Aid Form (FAF) is not acceptable. Students may be asked to complete supplemental documentation, but the university provides the needed forms to application filers.

Berkeley offers world-recognized academic excellence to a group of magnificently diverse students. The financial aid program supports this excellence and diversity. It invites outstanding students from all backgrounds to apply for admission and financial aid.

University of California at Berkeley is a four-year public university for men and women, located in Berkeley, California.

ROLLINS COLLEGE

"What are merit scholarships? Do many colleges offer them?"

David G. Erdmann
Dean of Admission and Financial Aid

New eligibility requirements for federally sponsored Guaranteed Student Loans have sparked a wave of discussion about the difficulty of paying for a college education. With tuition fees increasing far faster than the annual cost-of-living index, many parents and students who don't qualify for need-based financial aid are worried. For some families at least, relief may exist in the form of merit, or academic, scholarships.

Merit scholarships are not new to American higher education. In fact, before the College Scholarship Service was founded in the 1960s, awarding of scholarships bore no relationship to a student's need for funds. Colleges awarded aid to students in whom they were interested. After World War II, even the federal government adopted the merit principle by establishing the G.I. Bill, which provided free higher education to any veteran accepted at a college, regardless of need.

A rapid increase in the birthrate after the war ensured full beds and quality students for most colleges by the 1960s, and the nation's attention turned to helping disadvantaged youth. Colleges and universities focused their financial resources on students whose access to higher education was restricted. The College Scholarship Service's need analysis system provided a mechanism for identifying the financially needy. Although merit awards persisted throughout the period, they were limited to athletes and those with special talents.

In the late 1960s and early 1970s, the federal government also made major commitments to the needy, with programs such as the Basic Educational Opportunity Grant and National Defense Loans to supplement aid from colleges. With the influx of these federal funds, institutional resources were freed up, and colleges once again began offering merit awards as a means of competing for desirable students.

By the early 1980s the merit scholarship had become a standard recruitment tool at many colleges. In one survey conducted by Porter and McColloch in 1984, 83 percent of the responding colleges reported the use of merit awards. In another survey conducted by the College Board and National Association of Student Financial Aid Administrators the same year, 85 percent of the four-year private colleges and 90 percent of the four-year public colleges responding stated that they offered some awards on an academic basis without regard to financial need.

The increased use of academic merit awards by colleges and universities has pros and cons. Those in favor argue that the awards entice young people to excel, raise the academic status of an institution by attracting candidates with outstanding records, and help middle-class students who have little access to financial aid funds. Merit scholarships also allow private institutions to compete with the less expensive public colleges, to recognize accomplishment, and to reward excellence.

Those against merit awards argue that they deplete an already inadequate fund base, encourage students to play one institution against another, and erode the principle that students should select colleges on the basis of educational considerations rather than financial inducements. Admission to a selective college, they contend, should be recognition enough of academic excellence. Putting a dollar value on intellect and learning confuses the college selection process.

In spite of the outspoken critics of academic merit awards, there is every indication that these awards will continue. According to the National Center for Education Statistics, by 1995 the number of eighteen-year-olds will have declined to 3.3 million from a high of 4.3 million in 1979. Although this trend will begin to reverse itself after 1995, the resulting increase will be among minority groups that traditionally have not gone to college. Ninety-two percent of the institutions in the Porter and McColloch study reported that they award merit scholarships either to recognize and reward excellence or to recruit the best and the brightest. And 90 percent of the respondents said they would not eliminate their merit scholarship programs even if their competitors did. Obviously, these institutions believe such programs attract quality students who might otherwise attend other colleges.

How effective are merit scholarships in influencing students' choices? A 1984 study conducted for the College Board concluded that even a full-tuition scholarship had only a marginal effect on college choice for students who did not need financial aid. Many students, of course, do not fall into this category. Still, recent studies show that college quality, reputation, and prestige are the most important factors in the college choice process. Financial considerations are of secondary importance.

Despite these studies, colleges have obviously decided that merit scholarships are warranted. Faced with a declining number of high school graduates and convinced that highly qualified students increase an institution's perceived academic quality, most public and private colleges are using merit aid as a recruitment tool.

Rollins College, for instance, has a number of merit scholarships available to entering students. While the majority of these are awarded on the basis of academic excellence, many are offered to students who have contributed significantly to their schools or communities or who have outstanding talents in fields such as drama or music.

In 1984, Gary Jones, under secretary of education, proposed federally funded Learning for Leadership Grants designed to set standards, raise aspirations, and inspire our youth to improve their talents. Although the federal government has not responded to this call for merit awards, various states and organizations have. Florida awards up to $2,500 annually to resident secondary school students who have achieved a certain academic level and who attend any public or private college or university in the state. Other states have similar programs. The National Merit Corporation is probably the best known of the organizations that reward academic achievement, although only about one-third of the more than $18 million awarded annually by the corporation is given without regard to financial need.

The criticism of merit scholarships—that they are economically threatening to institutions and erode the principle of learning for learning's sake—continues. Clearly, however, merit scholarships are here to stay.

Rollins College is a four-year private liberal arts college for men and women, located in Winter Park, Florida.

PENNSYLVANIA STATE UNIVERSITY

> "Our soccer player has started for four years and been All-State for two years. Last year the team won both division and conference. Will all this help get him into college?"

Scott F. Healy
Assistant Vice President
and Director of Admission

Andrew J. Burgess
Admission Assistant

There's a face-off ahead for all aspiring student athletes. High school victories strengthen the determination many students have for taking their talents to the playing fields and classrooms of America's universities, and the dreams of many students include winning careers with the pros. College-bound athletes are placed in a menacing arena where every decision is a contest. Simply playing the "away" team pales in comparison to the Olympic-sized pressures placed on the student athlete. On the field, in the classroom, and on the home turf where recruitment begins, the student must stand strong and face an opponent that embodies the machinery of the competitive world of sports.

This machinery is a legion on the offensive, with each party jockeying for a key position. High school coaches are out to launch a shining star. College recruiters are looking for a player who can bring home the gold. Sportswriters are searching for their next feature. Teachers are demanding proof of the player's intellect. Friends and peers are judging the player's character. Parents are hoping for the best. Least of all are the self-imposed expectations of the player, who must grapple with ambition and the reality of his or her situation.

A virtual monster stands before the student athlete, but through the agility of thoughtful planning, careful counsel, and a realistic vision of the future, this larger-than-life "opponent" can be tamed. Indeed, the forces at play are all *components* that can further the success of the student athlete. The athlete, however, must balance his or her life and must take control of play *and* study. Success demands a sensible relationship between two collegiate worlds—academics and sports.

Craig James, who is now a running back for the New England Patriots, once described to us the number-one pressure facing high school All-Americans as they enter college: Prove to the world and yourself that you are truly an All-American among All-Americans. Recognition generally takes two full years of successful competition, and less than 2 percent achieve All-American status while in college. When reaching for such an elusive trophy, many students allow their academic priorities to slip to a distant second.

This is unfortunate. Athletic heroes are a minority; successful graduates are not. Parents should help their sons and daughters make realistic decisions concerning a college career. For the gifted student athlete, the monies are in hand for both an education *and* a chance at fame. Financial aid, however, is not a prize; it is merely a ticket to an education. The real prize is a college diploma. Appreciation for financial assistance means keeping a level head and not allowing the enchantment of athletics to eclipse academic performance.

Before yielding to any tempting financial aid packages, student athletes and their parents should consider the range of opportunities available at various institutions, both in athletics and academics. They should also learn the rules governing fair play. The official source for this information is the NCAA *Guide for the College-Bound Student Athlete*, which can be obtained by writing directly to the National Collegiate Athletic Association, Nall Avenue at Sixty-third Street, P.O. Box 1906, Mission, Kansas 66201. By understanding the rules of the

NCAA, parents and their students athletes will be better prepared to make informed and responsible decisions. In addition, by understanding recruiting policies and procedures, they will have a more realistic idea of the kinds of assistance and support available.

The *NCAA Guide* is very specific about the financial aid a student athlete may and may not receive. Among the forms of financial aid that a student *may* receive are the following:

- Unearned athletically related financial aid administered by the institution at which the student matriculates.
- Nonathletic grants for educational purposes and income from employment.

Both forms are subject to a very important stipulation: Assistance cannot exceed the current costs of attending an institution. Parents should be wary of any financial aid packages that go beyond this limit. Among the forms of financial aid that a student may *not* receive are the following:

- Athletically related financial aid to attend an institution's summer term before initial enrollment as a regular student.
- Athletically related financial aid administered by any source other than the institution at which the student matriculates.
- Any extra benefit not available to other students.

In essence, the NCAA rules strongly imply that a student athlete is a student, first and foremost. Athletic ability is a gift that can open the doorway to higher education. That doorway should be no different for a nonathlete. In the case of the athlete, however, special monies are available to defray the cost of a college education. Those monies are in no way meant to create a varsity elite with extraordinary campus privileges. Athletes should walk *with* the student body, not apart from it. A true college experience is not limited to the playing fields and locker rooms. It extends across the campus.

During the recruitment season, students will look to their parents for support and guidance. In preparation, wise families will seek out intelligent counsel and will discuss their children's goals for college and beyond. The face-off ahead should not be entered before rating the other players. Families should identify the recruiters for what they really are and should plan how best to stand up to them.

The pressure student athletes face cannot be eliminated, but it can be tackled with good sense and confidence. As in any endeavor, the participants need to recognize each other, understand the rules governing fair play, and keep in sight the actual, obtainable rewards. In college, the real winners are the students who leave their alma maters with a solid education and security for the future.

Pennsylvania State University is a four-year public university for men and women, located in University Park, Pennsylvania.

Sample Student Loan Application

On the next page is a sample student loan application from the New York State Higher Education Services Corporation in Albany, New York. State loans pay for full-time college study and must be repaid. All states also have full-time grant programs, which are awards that do not have to be repaid. New York, Vermont, and Minnesota are the only states that have need-based grant programs for *part-time* college study; students in these three states, especially adults in continuing education programs, now can get aid to pay for part-time course loads while they work to support themselves and their families.

The Financial Aid Hurdle

STUDENT LOAN APPLICATION
HE 100 (11/86)
WARNING: Any person who knowingly makes a false statement or misrepresentation on this form is subject to penalties which include fines or imprisonment under the U.S. Criminal Code and USC 1097

NEW YORK STATE HIGHER EDUCATION SERVICES CORPORATION
99 WASHINGTON AVENUE, ALBANY, NEW YORK 12255

IMPORTANT: TURN OVER AND READ INSTRUCTIONS CAREFULLY BEFORE COMPLETING **PRINT CAREFULLY**

PART A STUDENT / **PRINT OR TYPE**

1 Social Security Number | HESC USE ONLY | 2 Birth date — Mo Day Yr | 3 Area Code/Phone Number | 4 U.S. Citizenship Status — 1 Citizen 2 Eligible Non-citizen

5 Have you been a legal resident of NYS for 12 months immediately prior to the beginning of the academic period of this loan? — 1 YES 2 NO

6 Period Covered by this loan — MO YR MO YR — From To

Alien Registration Number

7 Name (Last) (First) (M.I.)

8 Are You Applying For (Check one) — 1 GSL ONLY 2 GSL AND SLS(ALAS) 3 SLS(ALAS) ONLY

9 Permanent Home Address Number and Street

City State Zip Code

10 REQUESTED LOAN AMOUNT $

11 Do you currently have a student loan guaranteed by New York State? (NYHEAC or NYSHESC) Check one 1 Yes 2 No

12 Have you received a Guaranteed Student Loan or SLS(ALAS) Loan from another State or Agency? — 1 Yes 2 No

If yes, complete these boxes — If the answer is no proceed to Item 13

GSL | SLS (ALAS) | Name of State or Agency | Amount borrowed from other State or Agency during this academic period | Total Amount owed | Interest Rate

13 Lender Name & Address

14 REFERENCES — (REFERENCES MUST RESIDE IN THE UNITED STATES) SEE INSTRUCTIONS

Nearest Living Adult Relative

Name (A)
Address City
State Zip Telephone No.
Relationship to Applicant
Employer Telephone No.

Nearest Living Adult Relative Not Residing at Address in Item 14 A.

Name (B)
Address City
State Zip Telephone No.
Relationship to Applicant
Employer Telephone No.

Promissory Note for a Student Loan Guaranteed by NYSHESC

I Promise To Pay I, the undersigned student borrower identified in Part A, Item 7, promise to pay to you or your order when this note becomes due as set forth in Paragraph II, the sum of

15 Requested Loan Amount—Must be the Same as Item 10 DOLLARS ($ .00)

or such loan amount as is advanced to me and identified to me in the Notice of Loan Guarantee and Disclosure Statement, plus interest as set forth in Paragraph III, and any other charges which may become due as provided in Paragraph VI. If I fail to pay any of these amounts when they are due. I will pay all charges and other costs, including the fees of an outside attorney and court costs that are permitted by Federal law and regulations for the collection of this loan, which you incur in collecting this loan (See Paragraphs II, III, VI on the other side.) My signature certifies that I have read, understood and agreed to the conditions and authorizations stated in the "Borrower Certification" printed on the reverse side

I UNDERSTAND THAT THIS IS A PROMISSORY NOTE. I WILL NOT SIGN THIS PROMISSORY NOTE BEFORE READING IT INCLUDING THE WRITING ON THE REVERSE SIDE. EVEN IF OTHERWISE ADVISED. I AM ENTITLED TO AN EXACT COPY OF THIS PROMISSORY NOTE. THE NOTICE OF LOAN GUARANTEE AND DISCLOSURE STATEMENT AND ANY AGREEMENT I SIGN. BY SIGNING THIS PROMISSORY NOTE I ACKNOWLEDGE THAT I HAVE RECEIVED AN EXACT COPY HEREOF.

16 Student Borrower Signature 17 Date

NOTICE TO STUDENT:
Terms of the Promissory Note continue on the reverse side.

PART B SCHOOL

18 NYSHESC SCHOOL CODE (USE STAMP)

19 NAME OF SCHOOL
ADDRESS Street City
State Zip Code Telephone No.

20 ANTICIPATED DATE OF PROGRAM COMPLETION — Month Year

21 DEPENDENCY STATUS — 1 Independent 2 Dependent

22 CLASS YEAR (Check only one) — Undergraduate or equivalent: 1 Fr 2 So 3 Jr 4 Sr 5 5yr — Graduate or Professional: 6 1yr 7 2yr 8 3yr 9 4yr 0 5yr

23 ACADEMIC PERIOD OF LOAN (Use Numbers) — Month Year Month Year — From To

24 Adjusted Gross Income $ | 25 Estimated Cost of Attendance for Loan Period $ | 26 Estimated Financial Aid for Loan Period $ | 27 Expected Family Contribution $ | 28 Enrollment Status — 1 Full-time 2 Half-time

My signature certifies that I have read and agreed to the conditions given in the "School Certification" printed on the REVERSE of this application

29 SIGNATURE OF AUTHORIZED SCHOOL OFFICIAL
30 PRINT OR TYPE NAME AND TITLE — Mo Day Yr
31 DATE

PART C LENDER

32 NYSHESC LENDER CODE

33 LENDER NAME, ADDRESS AND TELEPHONE NUMBER

34 SIGNATURE OF AUTHORIZED LENDING OFFICIAL

35 AMOUNT LENDER APPROVES $

LENDER COPY (ORIGINAL)

PRINT OR TYPE NAME AND TITLE

Date

0 1 2 3 4 5 6 7 8 9

Reprinted with the kind permission of the New York State Higher Education Services Corporation, Albany, New York.

Special Schools
and Programs for
Special Students

> *"To be nobody-but-yourself—in a world which is doing its best, night and day, to make you everybody else—means to fight the hardest battle which any human being can fight; and never stop fighting."*
>
> —e. e. cummings

As they investigate colleges, some students consider attending special schools instead of the garden-variety coed institution. In this chapter, the admission directors counsel women and minorities about the benefits of attending all-women's or all-minority colleges. They also look into alternative education programs for students who want to enjoy a special style of education as their college experience, and they advise parents of learning disabled students about how to select colleges.

Reasons for choosing an all-women's college tend to be very personal. Although an all-women's college is certainly not the right place for every woman, Elizabeth Vermey and Debra Thomas of Bryn Mawr and Aline Rivers of Spelman College make a strong case for such schools. If your daughter is considering making this choice—and you never even thought of going to an all-women's or all-men's school when you were a senior—read what these admission professionals have to say before you talk to your daughter. Her happiness isn't guaranteed by repeating your college experience.

If your family is black, Hispanic, Asian, or another minority, you and your teen need to be aware of certain trends in higher education across the country. Overall, college enrollments for black and Hispanic students have dropped during the past few years, and half of all minority students in college today are enrolled in two-year institutions. Furthermore, according to the Hoover Institution, a think tank in Stanford, California, Asian-American students, despite their academic qualifications, are having a more difficult time than are white candidates in getting into top colleges.

After college graduation, very few minorities, particularly blacks and Hispanics, are pursuing advanced degrees. In 1985, for instance, colleges in the United States awarded about forty-five hundred doctoral degrees to graduates in the physical sciences, and *USA Today* and the *New York Times* report that only forty-nine of those degrees went to minority students. In 1987, of the seventy thousand graduate students who earned master's degrees in business administration, only 3.6 percent were black and only 1.3 percent were Hispanic. According to the Graduate Management Admission Council, sponsor of the exam required for admission to most graduate schools of business, it is difficult to increase minority enrollment in MBA programs because there are so few minority mentors to encourage undergraduates to go on.

With good counseling, Patricia Carver of Stockton emphasizes, minority students can approach the college selection process with confidence, assured that there are many opportunities available to them. If your teenager is a bright minority student, he or she will probably be the target of numerous recruiting campaigns. Colleges are in fierce competition with one another for talented minority students, and they are continually developing new strategies to attract them to their campuses. Some schools, for instance, now sponsor special recruiting weekends. Most of these weekends are planned with the help of minority undergrads who have a special interest in seeing more minorities on their campuses. The undergrads serve as hosts and tour guides for the visiting students. The weekend at Dartmouth, called "Experience Dartmouth," has been particularly successful. As many as 83 percent of the accepted students who participate in the weekend program enroll in the college. Colleges are also recruiting more vigorously at racially and ethnically diverse high schools and are asking minority alumni to recommend promising candidates. In addition, schools like Amherst, Princeton, Morehouse, and Spelman are teaming up and sponsoring joint college nights to recruit minorities. These college nights give students a chance to compare programs right on the spot and give colleges a chance to address a larger audience.

Colleges are developing new minority recruiting strategies all the time. In 1987, for example, Columbia University announced that it will help its minority undergraduates pay off their college loans if they go on to earn doctoral degrees. If they earn their doctoral degrees at Columbia, the university will pay off three-quarters of their loans; if they earn their doctoral degrees at other institutions, the university will pay off one-half of their loans. The program is designed to increase the number of minority professors and thus the number of mentors and role models for minority students at colleges and universities. Be alert for these and other new minority recruiting efforts, and take advantage of them!

Whatever your teen's college preference—all-women's college, minority college, alternative education program—there are many alternatives to choose from. One is *right* for your son or daughter.

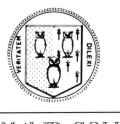

BRYN MAWR COLLEGE

> ## "We're not sure our daughter should attend an all-women's college. Will she get a good education there?"

Elizabeth G. Vermey
Director of Admission

Debra J. Thomas
Director of Public Information

If your daughter is a young woman with career aspirations, she may be having a difficult time choosing the right college. Besides the usual choices her male peers have—public or private, urban or rural, large or small—a young woman has several other things to consider that make a difference in her college education. For instance, recent research has found that bright female students who considered themselves outstanding in high school thought they were only average after their freshman year in college. Yet male students who saw themselves as above average in high school saw themselves in the same way after one year of college. Recent studies by the Association of American Colleges have also shown that in many coeducational classes female students are called on less often than male students, interrupted more frequently when they are talking, and given less feedback about their abilities.

About these findings a *Washington Post* editorial stated: "Probably at no other time in this century . . . have American women had both the career opportunities and the challenges in their personal lives that

205

they face today. For many, college is their last chance to train for that challenge. The last thing they need is a college experience that leaves them with diminished expectations and a diminished sense of their own value."

Do young women have an alternative to this kind of college experience? Absolutely. Women's colleges give female students every opportunity to excel and to prove themselves as leaders both in and out of the classroom. They foster a sense of self-worth and prepare women not only to enter the work force but also to compete with men on an equal footing. A senior at Barnard described her experience at an all-women's college in this way: "I was taught that I can do anything." A graduate from Bryn Mawr said: "A women's college encourages women to succeed and to overcome the myth that men achieve and women don't. At Bryn Mawr, my teachers expected me to take responsibility for my education. I had to work independently and participate in all class discussions."

Because women's colleges encourage female students to develop and demonstrate their leadership abilities, alumnae of women's colleges are more likely than are graduates of coeducational schools to enter fields traditionally dominated by men (at Bryn Mawr, women major in physics *twenty times* more often than the national average!). They are also more likely to go on to graduate and professional schools and to earn citations in *Who's Who*.

In 1985, the Women's College Coalition conducted a study of five thousand graduates from women's colleges of the classes of 1967 and 1977. The findings of the study, called " '67/'77: A Profile of Recent Women's College Graduates," are dramatic:

- ❏ Eighty-one percent of those surveyed went to graduate school.
- ❏ Forty-three percent of those employed have careers in law, medicine, computer science, and other "male" professions.
- ❏ Twenty-eight percent of those employed who graduated in 1967 earn more than $35,000 a year. (Among all working women who graduated from college in 1967, *only 8 percent* earn more than $35,000.)

Of course, women's colleges do have one obvious disadvantage: social life may be more difficult than at coeducational schools. However, many women's colleges have agreements with coeducational institutions close by, and the students from both kinds of schools take advantage of the arrangement. Bryn Mawr, for example, has a consortium with Swarthmore and Haverford colleges and with the University of Pennsylvania.

Today there are more than 110 women's colleges in the United States for young women to choose from. Here are just a few:

- Stephens College, Missouri (independent)
- Pine Manor, Massachusetts (two-year college)
- Barnard, Bryn Mawr, Mount Holyoke, Smith, Wellesley (the "sisters" colleges)
- St. Mary's College, Indiana
- Sophie Newcomb College, Louisiana (oldest coordinate institution in the United States; associated with Tulane University)
- Salem College, North Carolina
- Spelman College, Georgia (founded in 1881 to educate former slave women)
- Mills College, California (oldest college west of the Rocky Mountains)

Because there are usually more women in positions of authority at women's colleges than at coeducational institutions—as professors, administrators, presidents, trustees—young students learn from these role models what it takes to be professionals. Women's colleges prepare young women to live full lives—with careers *and* marriage, jobs *and* children. They offer seminars and internships with working women so that students can learn firsthand what it will be like to try to balance the demands of the home and the workplace. Some even offer courses to prepare seniors to cope with the pressures they'll face after college.

At women's colleges, women come first—in everything they do. For this reason—and for the many advantages they offer—women's colleges are a worthwhile choice for bright young women who are planning a successful future.

Bryn Mawr College is a four-year private university and liberal arts college for women, located in Bryn Mawr, Pennsylvania.

SPELMAN COLLEGE

> "Do schools with limited populations handicap graduates? Our daughter is thinking about attending a private college for black women."

Aline A. Rivers
Acting Dean of Students

In recent years I have often been asked the question "With decreasing enrollments among black students at colleges, what is the advantage of an academically talented black female attending a historically black private college for women?"

There is considerable concern throughout the country about the fact that black enrollments have declined at the college level. This decline is particularly distressing to the black community because, according to U.S. Bureau of Census figures, the number of black high school graduates has increased. These statistics indicate that access for minorities to higher education is a significant problem. The fact that the income of black families has lagged behind that of white and Hispanic families is a possible cause of the decline in black student enrollment at colleges. Another possible cause is the decrease in student financial aid.

This background information is important to keep in mind in a discussion of the viable choices for the academically talented black female student. Some parents question the role of any women's college today—whether predominantly white or black—in a world where women have to work alongside men. But advocates of women's colleges point out that these institutions play a vital role: They give women the chance to grow politically, socially, and intellectually, uninhibited by the presence of men. They draw women out of themselves and encourage them to achieve positions of leadership. And, according to the Women's College Coalition, a clearinghouse for information about women's colleges, they provide women with more opportunities for internships and career programs than many coed institutions do.

Black colleges play an equally vital role. In the first place, as an article in the 28 January 1987 edition of *The Philadelphia Inquirer* put it, there is a "growing perception among educators that black students generally experience greater intellectual and emotional growth on predominantly black campuses." In the second place, the cost of attending a historically black private college has remained consistently below the national average cost of attending other four-year private colleges. In the third place, black private colleges continue to provide financial aid to more than half of their students.

I can think of several additional reasons for attending a black women's college today. Spelman College, one such institution, offers the able young black student and her family all of the following advantages:

- ❑ The opportunity to live and grow with other black women in a nurturing environment.
- ❑ Participation in the "black experience." Students who have previously attended predominantly white schools often cite this as a benefit.
- ❑ An education that will lead to interesting and financially rewarding employment immediately after college.
- ❑ The opportunity to experience a full social life. Spelman belongs to the Atlanta University Center, a group of historically black colleges including all-male Morehouse and coed Clark and Morris Brown, as well as the graduate schools of Atlanta University, the Morehouse School of Medicine, and the Interdenominational Theological Center. Additionally, Spelman women interact socially with

students from Georgia Tech, Georgia State University, Emory University, and other institutions of higher education in the Atlanta area.

☐ Networking contacts that enhance the student's social, civic, and professional life. The Career Planning and Placement Office provides opportunities for students to acquire field experiences related to their academic programs and career interests. The Spelman Alumnae Student Externship Program affords students the unique advantage of visiting professional black women involved in law, health care, business, communications, and administration. The Student Internship Program enables students to obtain practical, in-depth experience in their chosen career fields.

☐ A degree that is highly respected and that will help the student gain admission to top graduate and professional schools.

Spelman College provides students with a unique learning environment through the Living-Learning Program, a holistic approach to the liberal education of students, which is designed to integrate residential education with the academic curriculum. Through small-group discussions in residence halls, panel debates, seminars, and convocations, students are stimulated to become more curious about global as well as curricular issues and are given forums for discussing their perspectives on these issues. Special emphasis is placed on developing faculty-student mentor relationships and leadership skills by providing role models from all sectors of society. Recent participants in the Living-Learning Program have included such eminent people as author Alice Walker; the Honorable Shirley Chisholm; the Honorable Andrew Young, mayor of Atlanta; and Dr. Ruth Perry, ambassador to Ghana.

Spelman College also provides an academic and social environment that enables women to become self-confident as well as culturally and spiritually enriched. This educational experience reinforces a sense of pride and hope, develops character, inspires the love of learning, and helps black women develop into leaders.

Spelman College is a four-year private liberal arts college for women, located in Atlanta, Georgia.

STOCKTON STATE COLLEGE

> ## "As a minority, how can our child get the best guidance on getting into college?"

Patricia Hall Carver
Director of Admission

As an admission director, I would not make a distinction between minority and majority advice. I would counsel minority students the same way I would counsel other students—with a good deal of love and empathy. Our youth need to be educated and nurtured in order to make their way in today's career-oriented society. They need parents, teachers, and counselors to share information and experiences that will help them meet their needs, whether academic, social, or psychological. Every child wants to be listened to. With this in mind, let me share a personal history with you.

Twenty years ago, Ann, a young black woman about to graduate from high school, received a rejection letter from the one college to which she had applied. Ann had applied to only one school because of the advice she had received earlier that year from the guidance counselor responsible for seniors. This man's advice was quite simple: "Ann, you are not college material. You are talented, however, so why not pursue a career in singing?" Ann was confused by this advice because she had performed well academically throughout high school.

211

She was also disappointed because she had hoped that her one and only meeting with her counselor would produce at least a few options for her future.

Without being informed about how to search for colleges, Ann wrote to a reputable music school that she had heard about in New York City. She requested an application and eagerly filled out and submitted it. After taking several tests and participating in a rigorous audition, she waited patiently—alone—for the results. Finally, she received a letter from the school informing her that, although she was talented, she unfortunately lacked the requisite training in piano and music theory, courses that had not been offered at her high school. Feeling defeated, Ann began to think that perhaps her counselor was right—perhaps she was not college material, after all. Ignorant of other options that might be available to her and reluctant to expose herself to further rejection, Ann lost her enthusiasm for pursuing a college education and decided to accept things as they were.

After she graduated from high school, Ann secured a summer job as a playground supervisor. She was content with the position until one of the community workers suggested that she might attend the local community college. Ann was excited by the prospect but feared that she would not be able to afford to go to school. The community worker assured her that most of her college expenses would be covered by a newly formed state program called the Educational Opportunity Fund. Buoyed by this news and grateful for her colleague's advice and encouragement, Ann not only enrolled in school but inspired her older sister, her mother, and other members of her family to attend college, too. And so began a family tradition.

There is a valuable lesson to be learned from Ann's experience: Guidance doesn't always come from traditional role models, and traditional role models don't always give the best advice. By being open and receptive, one can get help in the most unlikely ways.

As parents, you need to be aware of the many possibilities for effective counseling that are available to you and your child. By all means make the most of the services of school guidance counselors, but don't limit yourselves or your teen to them. Schools are overcrowded, and guidance counselors have so much administrative paperwork to fill out that they have little time to perform the tasks for which they were trained.

Parental involvement with the high school is a must. Join the

PTA. Volunteer your services both at school and in the community. Make your interest in counseling services known to your school board. Show your concern. For your teen to receive effective counseling when he or she needs it, you must work together with guidance counselors and classroom teachers. Commitment is the key: Ask questions, be available, follow up, don't give up, and share your experiences with other parents.

Winston Churchill once said that education ought to be about teaching people the skills they need to do three things: understand the world, enjoy the world, and contribute to the world. Let's support our children and our schools by making sure we know what services are provided and what people are responsible for providing them.

Stockton State College is a four-year public liberal arts college for men and women, located in Pomona, New Jersey.

MASSACHUSETTS INSTITUTE OF TECHNOLOGY

> ## "Our son wants to major in engineering but his SAT scores as a junior aren't very strong. What can he do *now* to strengthen his chances of acceptance?"

Anthony Canchola-Flores
Assistant Director of the Office of Minority Education

Minority students interested in mathematics and science who would like to strengthen those interests have an opportunity to do so during the summer at the Massachusetts Institute of Technology (MIT). What better setting than a major research-oriented institution with an excellent reputation in mathematics and science? For the past twelve years, the Minority Introduction to Engineering and Sciences (MITES) program has attracted and enrolled minority students nationwide. This six-week summer program gives promising minority students a taste of the opportunities available in the fields of engineering and science.

MIT's MITES program is similar to programs at other U.S. universities and is part of the nationwide Minority Introduction to Engineering (MITE) model that was developed by the Engineers'

Council for Professional Development. The council responded to the underrepresentation of minorities in the engineering and science professions by enlisting the support of a variety of industries and establishing MITE programs at forty U.S. campuses. Although the MITE programs all have the same purpose, they vary in length and curriculum from campus to campus.

Our MITES program at MIT is designed for students who have completed their junior year in high school, though promising sophomores are sometimes accepted. Admission criteria include academic performance, PSAT results, a personal essay about the student's interest in mathematics and science, and letters of recommendation from mathematics and science instructors. Students who are accepted by the selection committee focus their energies on pursuing an education in science or engineering.

The MIT MITES program is sponsored and administered by the dean's office in the College of Engineering. Over the years, it has grown from a two-week residential program to its present six-week format. MITES students enroll in mathematics, physics, biochemistry, electronics, humanities, and design classes. They also participate in career-oriented seminars to discuss their career options and to interact with minority role models.

Our MITES program has introduced a large number of talented minority undergraduates to MIT. Although the program wasn't intentionally developed as a recruitment vehicle, many of our MITES students do end up enrolling at MIT. In 1985, for instance, our admission office reports that twelve MITES students enrolled at MIT; in 1986, twenty-three enrolled; and in 1987, nineteen enrolled.

High school students who enter the MITES program typically take the SAT and one or more Achievement Tests before the beginning of their senior year in high school. Even if a student doesn't do well on these exams, an outstanding MITES record will still generally give him or her a better chance of being accepted to MIT.

High school students who want to improve their chances of acceptance to MIT should investigate not only MITES but also Upward Bound and other academic support programs that are available nationwide. Parents and high school guidance counselors who recognize a student's academic problems or low test scores early enough can help the student improve his or her high school performance. Of course, no enrichment program at this institution or at any other offers a real guarantee of acceptance, but such programs can considerably improve a student's odds.

Our MITES program has a roster of outstanding alumni. Many have gone on to MIT and to other prestigious institutions for their undergraduate work. Typically, these students excelled during their MITES experience, improving their study habits and developing new skills in science and mathematics that helped them during their senior year and later during their transition from high school to college. They also gained a new sense of self-confidence and self-reliance by examining their intellectual capacity and challenging their creativity in an intensely academic environment similar to the one they would find at MIT or at any other university.

Students who are interested in programs like the MITES program at MIT should talk to their guidance counselors early in their high school junior year. The MITES program gives the MIT Admission Office the opportunity to preview and recruit students. But more importantly, it shows minority students the challenges and rewards that a science and engineering education can hold for them.

Massachusetts Institute of Technology is a four-year private university for men and women, located in Cambridge, Massachusetts.

Organizations That Help Minority Students Academically and Financially

A Better Chance (ABC)
Leading talent search organization that helps minorities gain access to independent and public secondary schools.

Director of Programs
A Better Chance
419 Boylston Street
Boston, MA 02116

National Action Council for Minorities in Engineering (NACME)

Aims to increase the number of minorities who earn bachelor's degrees in engineering by offering an Incentive Grants Program, Summer Engineering Employment Project, Field Services, and publications for parents and students.

NACME
3 West Thirty-fifth Street
New York, NY 10001

National Scholarship Service and Fund for Negro Students (NSSFNS)

Acts as a clearinghouse for financial aid; provides tutorial services and educational, career, and financial aid counseling.

NSSFNS
Southeastern Regional Office
965 Martin Luther King, Jr., Drive NW
Atlanta, GA 30314

United Negro College Fund

Provides scholarships for undergrads who attend one of forty-two historically black colleges. Must be accepted first and then nominated by the college's financial aid director.

United Negro College Fund
500 East Sixty-second Street
New York, NY 10021

INROADS, Inc.

National career development organization that places and develops talented minority students (black, Hispanic, and native American) in business and industry. ▸

INROADS, Inc.
1221 Locust Street
Suite 410
St. Louis, MO 63103

ASPIRA of America, Inc.
An association of community-based organizations providing leadership, development, and educational services to Latino youth.

ASPIRA of America, Inc.
1112 Sixteenth Street NW, #2900
Washington, D.C. 20036

ST. JOHN'S COLLEGE

> "Our daughter is interested in some colleges with unconventional programs, but we're afraid they'll hurt her chances for graduate school. Aren't these schools just for artsy people?"

John Christensen
Director of Admission

In 1852, in a series of nine lectures, John Henry Newman set out to define the purposes and uses of education. "The Idea of a University" defended liberal arts education as an end in itself rather than as a means to some more pragmatic end. Newman's principles still underlie liberal arts education today, and his defenses might well be used against the pressure for preprofessional studies in colleges.

All colleges share as their goal the education of the individual, but the overarching concern of the liberal arts college is what Newman called "the trained intellect." For every liberal arts college, the study of liberal arts is its own end and its own reward. These institutions do not expect their graduates to have mastered all the fields they encountered as students. They do not even expect students to be masters of their major field. In fact, most graduates would agree that the content of a specific course such as calculus or medieval history was lost to them by their tenth class reunion. But the skills of analysis, the ability to think things through and develop alternative approaches and solutions, have remained and have stood them in far better stead than the ability to recall the shape of an asymptotic curve or the date of the Peasants' Revolt. At a liberal arts college, Newman said, a "habit of mind is formed that lasts for life." If the public's response is "Impractical!" then part of the vocation of these colleges must be to reeducate the public.

When one's goal is an electrical engineering degree, the curriculum is fairly well-defined and any good engineering school will offer the necessary courses. Liberal arts colleges, however, offer different ways to develop the "habit of mind" Newman talks about. Different liberal arts schools take different routes to this same goal, and usually the entire institution is shaped and defined by the path chosen. There is, thus, a distinctive flavor about individual liberal arts colleges. Some lay down a rather standard list of requirements and channel students into majors after their second year. Others—St. John's, for instance—lead students through a prescribed four-year program of reading. Still others do not require a major but urge students to explore a broad range of interdisciplinary studies. The freedom to study whatever appeals is a rare experience. If liberal education is to be a preparation of a state of mind, then it shouldn't be too narrow an experience.

Liberal arts colleges that offer something different often put greater responsibility on the students themselves to make their education fulfilling. At the same time, grades, evaluation, testing, and curricula are more likely to respect the individuality and uniqueness of each student. For example, grades at most schools are a letter or a number. These grades say something about what a student has done in a course, as compared to other students, but they say very little about the student's strengths and weaknesses. Schools like St. John's use narrative comments about students so that evaluations not only describe what has already been done, where the student's strengths lie, but also comment on what might still be done, where the student might improve.

Is a liberal arts education a disadvantage when students apply to graduate schools? No. Graduate schools do not seek narrowly prepared candidates. In fact, most medical schools don't want much more in science preparation than the required five courses; they prefer to teach their future doctors the more advanced material themselves. Pre-professional training is a myth because, as most employment studies suggest, very few individuals remain in a field directly related to their undergraduate majors. If college is to form a "habit of mind," then it must be left alone to do so, without the imposition of preprofessional courses whose content changes with changing times. College may be the last chance students have to enjoy *Twelfth Night* before they start reading the *Wall Street Journal* for the rest of their lives.

How does a student know if he or she will be happy at a liberal arts college that offers an alternative type of education? If a student finds high school dissatisfying, if the standard interaction of lecture and note taking seems incomplete, then an alternative educational setting may be in order. If a student feels like a number in a large system, then something with more personal responsibility and input may appeal. If a student wants intellectual challenge as part of the fabric of the academic environment, then a more intense educational system may be suitable. And if a student is drawn to a broad and diverse range of studies, then a school with minimal restrictions, few distribution requirements, and a progressive system may be a better fit.

Liberal arts colleges that offer alternative educational programs are not many but they are distinctive. Among others, they include St. John's College, Sarah Lawrence College, Hampshire College, Bard College, Bennington College, Brown University, Oberlin College, Colorado College, Wesleyan University, Evergreen State College, Antioch College, and New College of the University of South Florida. Though they vary in size, location, and philosophy, all of these schools have as their goal the "trained intellect." Each pursues that goal along its own distinctive path.

Choosing a college is a complicated process that warrants attention, care, and self-examination. If your teenager feels that what's right for the crowd is not right for him or her, then these colleges may be worth investigating.

St. John's College is a four-year private liberal arts college for men and women, located in Annapolis, Maryland.

COLORADO COLLEGE

> **"How does a college with special programs choose its applicants?"**

Richard Wood
Director of Admission

Some small liberal arts colleges have a specialness about them that influences their selection process in many ways. Colorado College is one of these.

In 1970 the college made a dramatic departure from the way students and teachers approach their course work, going from the traditional fifty-minute, three-meetings-a-week, many-subject schedule to a much simpler one called the Block Plan. Instead of semesters or quarters, Colorado College divides the year into three-and-a-half-week segments. During each of these segments, faculty and students alike focus on a single subject—professors teach only one course at a time and students take only one.

There is a certain intensity to it all. A semester of organic chemistry in less than a month? A year of intermediate French in seven weeks? Needless to say, the system demands that the student remain healthy, keep up with the course work, and attend class faithfully every day.

But the intensity consists more of momentum and immersion than pressure. Bells don't cut off discussions and lab experiments. The subject at hand comes to dominate the lives of the students and

222

teachers. Meeting hours and class structure suit the nature of the material instead of the other way around. An astronomy class can meet at midnight in the mountains (the air is clear out here); an English class can spend the morning reading a Shakespeare play aloud and team up in the afternoon with an acting class to try out a few scenes; a geology class can take a week-long field trip into the Rocky Mountains.

It may be because of the small classes, or the rapport that builds up between professors and students who see each other every single day, or the faculty's commitment to undergraduate teaching—but whatever the reason, students develop strong, close relationships with their teachers. Students have access to the entire faculty, not just to the teacher whose class they happen to be in. If they are working on a paper, preparing for an exam, or looking for a reaction to a poem or short story they have just written, they can call or drop in at professors' offices.

How does a college with this intense study format select its students? In the first place, a considerable amount of preselection takes place. Our typical candidates are attracted to Colorado College through their own research or by word of mouth and are not recruited in the usual sense. They tend to be bright, energetic young people who welcome the idea of throwing themselves wholeheartedly into a subject. They are not inclined to follow the crowd and don't need the prestige of attending an institution with a big name. They have a certain adventurousness, which brings over half of those who attend Colorado College more than a thousand miles from home.

These students are academic self-starters who like to explore and be challenged, who will participate in classroom discussions rather than hide in the forty-fourth row taking notes. Many come to Colorado College with certain already developed interests that lead them into independent study projects.

At the least, Colorado's Block Plan demands academic commitment, and candidates for admission best reveal this by the way they have handled their studies in high school. We favor those who take tougher rather than easier courses, who carry a fairly heavy load of classes (four or five per year), and who have balanced preparation in all academic areas (English, history, mathematics, foreign languages, and science). We also favor candidates who don't slack off during their senior year!

Although good grades are something we're used to seeing, they alone are not enough. The written part of the college application is just as important as the high school record. How effective is the candidate's writing? What kind of thought has been given to career and life goals? We admire candidates who seem to have done a few activities well enough to be very good at them rather than those who submit a long list of memberships in clubs, teams, and organizations. In fact, applicants who have achieved goals through persistence or dogged determination are likely to be a good match for the Block Plan, and we want them to be able to tell us why the things they do are important to them.

It is always a blessing to have high scores on college aptitude tests, but Colorado College has never allowed test scores to be the determining factor in an admission decision. We know that a high score generally reveals that a person is intelligent, but a low score may not be proof that a person lacks intelligence.

When we read through recommendations and ratings from teachers, counselors, and others, we look for clues that candidates may or may not be suited for the Block Plan at Colorado College. We pay close attention, therefore, when counselors, teachers, and other recommenders seem to know the college. We urge our candidates to give careful attention to selecting those who will write recommendations for them because these people can make a difference.

We are always impressed by students who appear to be running their own "getting-into-college" program. Conversely, we are wary of candidates whose parents are too involved. Students should initiate their own contacts with the college, make their own appointments, and do their own telephone follow-up. Parents need to be supportive partners in the process, of course, but it is the student who will attend Colorado College and perform under the Block Plan.

Our selection process may not appear to be different from other colleges. But students who come to Colorado College are different, so preselection clearly has a strong influence on the process. No doubt this accounts for the fact that very few freshmen are disappointed or surprised after they arrive on campus, even though they have had no previous experience quite like the Block Plan.

How do you know if the Block Plan is for you? The answer is you just do.

Colorado College is a four-year private liberal arts college for men and women, located in Colorado Springs, Colorado.

College Programs for the Learning Disabled

Parents of learning disabled teenagers worry about which colleges are best for their child. "Where will our daughter be most comfortable?" "Is there someone qualified at the college to help our son solve academic and social problems?"

Melissa Henry, Director of College Placement at the Forman School for the Learning Disabled in Litchfield, Connecticut, outlines two important steps that parents of learning disabled teens should take during their child's college selection process. The first involves helping their teen evaluate colleges based on his or her special needs. Many colleges have learning specialists to coordinate study skills programs and courses for learning disabled students. Parents can meet with these specialists to discuss their child's specific requirements. Parents and their teenager also can work with admission officers, program advisors, and professors to tailor courses, study facilities, and housing to their child's special situation. Some colleges offer first-semester transition courses and reduced course loads. In addition, they may provide special help with schedules, extra access to professors, and special study areas. Gathering this information beforehand is imperative as parents and teens evaluate colleges. Following up after acceptance is equally important.

The second step parents should take involves their teenager's college application. Melissa Henry helps Forman seniors decide whether or not to make their disability known to a college on their application. Revealing a learning disability is not necessary in every case, but specific needs should be made known so that the proper "fit" between student and school can be achieved. Colleges cannot ask about learning disabilities on their application forms, but a student may describe his or her disability in a letter and attach it to the form. Both the student and his or her parents should speak to the admission professionals at the college and should find out who will be reviewing the application. If a learning specialist will be reviewing it, the parents may want to have their child's psychoeducational evaluation and testing record sent to the college. *Who* looks at the student's application folder can mean the difference between acceptance and rejection.

Time and effort in investigating what a college offers, combined with strong college prep courses, can pay off in the right acceptance for any learning disabled student.

12

Acceptance: The Moment of Decision

"The difficulty in life is the choice."

—GEORGE MOORE

Believe it or not, things are beginning to come together. Your child is ready—the colleges have been chosen and visited, the tests taken, the essays written and carefully proofread, and the teacher's recommendations requested. All that's left is for your teen to complete the admission and financial aid applications, lick the stamps, and mail the envelopes. Together you have made most of the decisions. Now the colleges have their turn.

Before investing his or her future in this last step, your child should know about the various kinds of college acceptance: early admission, early decision, rolling admission, and traditional admission. Each acceptance method gives you options and has consequences. For example, early admission allows a bright student who is emotionally older than his or her peers to skip the senior year of high school and become a college freshman instead. Early decision requires a firm commitment to a single choice, and a conscientious applicant must think twice before applying. The admission directors in this chapter will guide you and your teen through the different acceptances, explain how they work, and counsel you about how to choose a method of acceptance.

After the applications arrive at the colleges and are reviewed by the admission staff, several things can happen. Of course, your teenager could be acccepted at his or her first-choice college and be ecstatic. But if your son or daughter is not accepted at that dream school, help your child think about how to deal with this situation gracefully and positively.

We've tried to put college acceptance—and rejection—into perspective. After being rejected by a prestigious Ivy, one student was so depressed and shaken that he didn't want to go to school and face his friends. His sky had fallen. He even lost interest in checking the mail each day for other acceptances. Then a counselor, who by coincidence had been in the same situation years back, suggested to him, "Turn the rejection into success somewhere else. You'll have professors to impress, clubs to join, and lasting relationships to make at a school that really wants you. Besides, there's nothing you can do about it."

Sometimes, instead of being rejected, a student may find he or she has been put on a favorite college's waiting list. If your teen is wait-listed, read what one admission director says to do next. Waiting to get off a wait list can be risky.

If your teen was rejected by a first-choice college last year, he or she may be in the position of applying to that school this year as a transfer candidate. One admission director told us about a student who was attending a large California university and wanted to transfer to the director's northeastern college. To improve her chances of acceptance, the applicant sent a videotape of her life in California along with her application. The unusual tape made its case creatively, with shots of a ski-loving freshman on the naked slopes of sunny hills and in oversized classes of four hundred students. With a strong freshman academic record and thoughtful, *specific* reasons for wanting to transfer to a particular, small, northern college, the applicant was accepted. In this chapter, the admission director at Georgetown University addresses the issue of transferring and tells you what chances transfers have of being accepted.

Most students who apply to several colleges have two or three acceptances to choose among. Sometimes this decision isn't as easy as it sounds. Given relatively equal academic and financial aid opportunities at different colleges, there's no crystal ball students can gaze into to see what life would be like at one school compared to another. Sometimes, a college choice is made without 100 percent conviction that it's the "right" and "only" decision, and the road not taken will always remain a mystery. No college is perfect. The college choice is more like an arranged marriage. Look for the best match now; love will come later.

NEW YORK UNIVERSITY

"We don't understand the different kinds of college acceptance. Which one should our child consider?"

David Finney
Director of Admission

Early admission, early decision, rolling admission, and *traditional admission* are terms that colleges use to describe the various admission and acceptance plans that they follow. Since each plan has its advantages and disadvantages, as well as its own timetable, students and their parents need to understand what these terms mean before applying to colleges.

The *early admission* plan offers students the chance to apply to college after their junior year and to complete the requirements for a high school diploma during their first year of college. The early admission option frequently appeals to highly motivated students who feel that they have realized the maximum benefit from high school. Since the traditional college counseling process usually does not begin until the spring of the junior year or fall of the senior year, early admission applicants should have a well-developed understanding of their educational goals by the time they are sophomores. Many professionals question the advantages of skipping the senior year experience

230

for a head start in college. Students should be certain that they are both academically and *emotionally* ready to begin college before they apply to schools under the early admission plan.

The *early decision* plan is designed for the student who has decided on a college early in the senior year. The deadline to apply usually falls in November, with admission decisions mailed out between mid-December and mid-January. Once offered admission under the early decision plan, a student *must* enroll. Therefore, the student must be certain that the college or university is his or her first choice. Because of the timetable involved, early decision is sometimes difficult for students who are required to audition or to submit portfolios. It also puts emphasis on the junior year, since senior grades are rarely available. If denied admission under the early decision plan, a student *may* be able to have his or her application reviewed again during the traditional admission process.

Early decision is a good choice for some students but not for others. Lauren for example, was seeking a particular type of theater program. During the summer before her senior year, she was able to visit a number of colleges that were recommended by her high school guidance counselor. She toured the campuses, interviewed admission counselors, and researched the theater departments and their offerings on her trip. By the beginning of September, Lauren felt certain that one college was her favorite. In October she visited that college again and reaffirmed that it was clearly her first choice. She decided to apply under the early decision plan, recognizing that, if accepted, she would attend and, if rejected, she would still have time to apply to other colleges under either traditional or rolling admission.

By contrast, Reuben wanted a traditional liberal arts program, but he wasn't sure what size, location, or learning environment was right for him. He thought that an early decision application to a popular big-name college would put him out of his misery and let him coast through his senior year. However, since his plans were not well formulated and his motives were not the wisest, Reuben's counselor discouraged him from using the early decision option.

The *rolling admission* plan allows students to file an application at a college up to one year prior to matriculation. Applications are reviewed as they are received and students are notified of a decision soon after they apply. Students offered admission usually have until

May 1 of the year in which they intend to enroll to notify the college of their decision.

Because of its flexibility, the rolling admission plan has some obvious advantages. Consider Ryan, for instance. As a senior, Ryan narrowed down his choices to the business programs at four colleges— his state university, which operated on the rolling admission plan, and three others. Although Ryan had not determined if State was his first choice, he preferred it to one of the other schools. He decided that if accepted at State under the rolling admission plan, he would apply to only two of the other three schools on his list. An early acceptance from State would let him know that a spot was reserved for him at one of his top three choices. As a result, he could be more relaxed about the admission process at the other two colleges. He would also have ample time to evaluate all of his options before committing himself to a final choice in May.

The *traditional admission* plan is the one followed by most colleges, with an application deadline typically falling between January and March of the senior year. The late deadline allows students to take full advantage of the fall months to visit colleges when classes are in session and to meet with admission counselors who come to their high schools. It also allows them to bolster their academic record with a strong performance during the first semester of their senior year.

Most students prefer the traditional admission plan because it gives them a little extra time to make their choices and to assemble their applications. Heather, for example, was interested in three colleges. Although she had visited all three, she had not been able to decide on a first, second, or third choice. Moreover, since she was planning to major in art and design, she felt that her portfolio would be better if she could add to it work from her senior art class. By applying under the traditional admission plan, she would have plenty of time to prepare her portfolio, and she could revisit the three colleges of her choice in the spring.

Each of the admission plans described above has advantages and disadvantages. Guidance counselors and admission representatives can help students and their parents better understand the specifics of each option.

Students should determine which colleges best meet their needs and then apply to those institutions. Each college will offer one or more admission plans. Each also will have an admission timetable with a number of crucial deadlines. Students should adhere strictly to those deadlines throughout the admission process.

New York University is a four-year private university for men and women, located in New York City.

BOWDOIN COLLEGE

> ## "How does 'early decision' acceptance work? Does applying for early acceptance have drawbacks our child should consider?"

William Mason
Director of Admission

A small number of colleges and universities offer applicants an opportunity to apply for college acceptance under a special arrangement called the early decision program. This program can resolve the matter of college acceptance earlier in the calendar year than the traditional program can. The attractiveness of such a program for certain families is that it removes the pressure and uncertainty of waiting until spring for a decision. Additionally, since few students can decide on a single college as early as the fall of their senior year, early decision appears to be a way to avoid competing in the larger spring applicant pools.

Two features that distinguish early decision from other admission programs are the timing of the application and the binding nature of the student's agreement. Early decision deadlines occur during the months of October and November of a student's senior year, with the institution guaranteeing that a decision will be forthcoming within a month or so. By applying under the early decision strictures, a student agrees that, if accepted, he or she will attend the institution and will file no other college applications.

There are three types of early decision that a college admission committee can make: acceptance, deferral, and refusal. Since it guarantees admission, acceptance, of course, is the ultimate goal of the early decision candidate. Deferral is more anguishing, and refusal can be downright devastating. Deferral means that the admission committee could not reach a consensus on the student's application. A student who receives a deferral notice is automatically released from early decision agreements, and his or her application is transferred to the regular process for a second review in the spring. Refusal usually means that, from an academic point of view, the candidate has applied to an institution unrealistically matched to his or her abilities.

Before applying for early decision acceptance, parents and their teenagers should seriously consider both the benefits and the drawbacks of the program. The benefits are fairly obvious. An early decision acceptance reduces the anxiety that tends to build between parents and students during the application process. It saves families the expense of multiple applications and campus visits. It frees students to enjoy the activities of senior year and may even encourage them to take intellectual risks or try new experiences. Finally, it brings great joy and relief to parents and students alike. As one senior put it, "I was relieved of the pressure of competing against my classmates for acceptance to colleges."

Though perhaps less obvious, the drawbacks of applying for early decision acceptance are equally worthy of consideration. First, since the grades, scores, and activities of senior year are unavailable, early decision acceptance relies heavily on a student's performance through the junior year. Second, since the early decision acceptance is binding, the student does not have the luxury of changing his or her mind. Some students who are accepted and agree to attend a certain college under the early decision program later have second thoughts. This is especially true of students who spend little time researching colleges and apply for early decision acceptance not because they are sure of their choice but because it seems easier to gain admission that way. As they hear their fellow students discussing other schools, they begin to regret their decision, and they may go off to college with many unresolved doubts. Last but not least, when early decision ends in deferral or refusal, rather than acceptance, it can undermine or destroy a student's confidence just at the time when the deadlines for applying for regular acceptance are approaching. One student was paralyzed by an early refusal: "What's the use of applying to other schools? I'm not going to get in anywhere!"

The early decision program is clearly not for everyone. Students who are interested in the program should be realistic; they should take a careful look at a school's rank-in-class figures and average test scores before they apply. They should be sure that the school offers all (or most) of the academic, extracurricular, and other options they are looking for. They should visit the school, walk around the campus, sample the social life, attend a class or two, talk to students and professors. Above all, they should feel that "this is the school for me!"

One counselor told of a senior who raced past her office early in September and breathlessly announced, "Oh, by the way, I'll be applying for early decision." The counselor agreed to get the student's file pulled together early and asked where the application was going. "I'm not sure which college yet," said the student, "but I'm definitely applying for early decision somewhere." This is early decision for all the wrong reasons.

For the student intent on carefully evaluating his or her educational needs and finding an institutional match, the early decision program tends to bring issues into focus earlier than normal. Much can be gained by early decision acceptance if a student is ready and committed to the decision.

Bowdoin College is a four-year private liberal arts college for men and women, located in Brunswick, Maine.

Choosing Among Several College Acceptances

Being accepted at several colleges may seem like a dream come true, but it can also be something of a dilemma.

Fall's choice of where to apply, though certainly difficult, is only tentative; spring's choice of where to attend is final. Since every college that accepts your child wants him or her to enroll, there may be some "courting," some invitations to receptions and other special events, and possibly even some pressure in the form of phone calls from coaches or alumni.

One good way your teen can prepare for this pleasant dilemma is to spend the time between application deadlines and April 15 doing more research on the schools on his or her list and ranking them in order of preference. Your child has matured significantly since the spring of the junior year when the college list was first made. A little more research now will avoid an April of crazed indecision.

"Revisiting schools is probably the best way to finalize a choice," says Susan Moriarty, college counselor at the Hopkins School in New Haven, Connecticut. "A school may feel very different to you when you know you can go there." The school itself may provide a bus trip or an "admitted students' day" to help teens decide. Some students have found that their "gut feeling" about a school is the most reliable basis for a decision. Others distrust it. Gayle Moskowitz, a counselor at Millburn High School, suggests that students visit the college on a weekend: "Classes are classes at many schools, but a weekend tells you if the cultural and recreational life is going to satisfy you." While your teen is visiting, he or she should be sure to look up a high school alumnus. Someone who's made the transition from Hometown High to Chosen College can explain more about "fit" than all the literature, admission personnel, and tour guides put together.

The most informed decision about which college to attend will be based on careful judgment at the beginning of the process, a good sense of self, first impressions, admission office information, the testimony of enrolled students, and firsthand research.

UNIVERSITY OF VERMONT

> ## "What is wait-listing? What are the *real* chances of being accepted off a wait list?"

Linda M. Kreamer
Director of Admission

Nowadays the process of applying for admission, especially to selective colleges, generates a considerable degree of uncertainty and anxiety in both students and parents. Probably no part of that process is more uncertain and anxiety-producing than the wait list. It may help to understand which colleges use wait lists and why and to know that the wait list is viewed as a necessary evil by many admission people. The wait list is a creation that no one really likes.

Wait lists are used by colleges that have more desirable applicants than they can accommodate. The job of the admission office is to select the most appropriate class of the most appropriate size for the college or university. "Bringing in" a class that is too large or too small will have serious implications for both the college and its students. Unfortunately, the business of predicting how many students will accept an offer of admission is uncertain. The wait list helps admission directors deal with that uncertainty. The term used most often by admission people in this context is *yield*.

Yield is the percentage of admitted students that enroll in a college. The number of offers of admission a college makes is determined by its predicted yield. (Even the most selective and highly regarded colleges do not enroll all of their admitted students.) Selective colleges and universities predict a yield that leaves some room for error. The wait list allows them to reserve a group of applicants who can be admitted if the initial number of responses to their offers is too small.

Nineteen eighty-seven was labeled by some as "the year of the wait list." Many colleges experienced a large increase in the number of applications they received that year, leading to speculation that individual students were applying to many more colleges and universities than usual. As a result, yield became especially difficult to predict and some wait lists grew in length. The fact that in many cases yield actually increased that year contributes to the feeling that predicting yield and controlling enrollment are becoming more and more difficult for the admission director.

Most admission directors will tell you that they hope to be able to accept some part of their wait list. There will be very strong applicants on the list whose interest in the college is sincere, and colleges are glad to be able to respond positively to that interest. On the other hand, it is not wise to predict a yield so low that extensive use of the wait list is assured. Every admission person knows of times when a college made offers of admission to its entire wait list and still was not able to fill its freshman class.

Knowing something about why colleges use wait lists still leaves the question of how a student should respond to a wait-list offer. It may help to realize that in one way the term *wait list* is a misnomer. A student is not well advised to "wait" for the results of a wait-list offer. It is critical that a student make sure he or she has a place at another college or university. This usually means paying a tuition deposit at another school by May 1. It is unusual for a college to offer admission to a student on its wait list before May 1. A student is well advised to consider carefully all actual offers of admission and to make a commitment to the college or university that seems like the best alternative. If an offer of admission from the wait-list school arrives after that commitment has been made, the first college will understand that the student's commitment has changed because of the wait-list offer. The deposit money, however, is not returned.

Nothing is more unpredictable about selective college admission than the chances of being accepted off a wait list. Many colleges and universities send detailed explanations of their wait-list policies with response letters. These explanations address such issues as the ranking of wait-list candidates, the timing of wait-list decisions, and the history of wait-list offers in recent years. Though helpful, this information is not a reliable indication of whether an offer of admission will be forthcoming in a particular year or not.

Students and parents in the process of applying to selective colleges may want to keep some advice about the wait list in mind. Realize that the wait list is a necessary, though undesirable, part of admission to selective colleges. If you apply to a highly selective college or university, your chances of being wait-listed are good. If you do receive a wait-list offer, don't wait to accept an offer from another school. Choose the best of your alternatives and make a deposit.

If you plan to stay on a college's wait list, read the information that arrives with your letter and follow whatever advice is offered. If you are encouraged to provide additional information, do so. Make sure that your current academic work and any recent developments in your life are well represented in your file. If your interest in the college or university is very strong, let the admission people know in a letter. Don't send balloon-a-grams to the dean or call the admission office every day. You won't get off the wait list any faster. And above all, don't follow the example of the student who was wait-listed at two schools and wrote letters to both of them promising that she would attend if admitted. Her conflicting promises were revealed when she mailed the letters in the wrong envelopes!

University of Vermont is a four-year public university for men and women, located in Burlington, Vermont.

What to Do If Your Teen Doesn't Get in Anywhere

The heart-chilling news passed around the senior class quickly. "Did you hear about John? He didn't get in *anywhere!*"

Once in a while, a student grossly miscalculates his or her qualifications and ends up in John's situation. Occasionally, even fairly realistic calculation can end in this result. The pool of applicants at any given school varies from year to year, and no one can predict in September what will happen in April. The world, however, does not come to an end when your child fails to gain admission to any of the colleges to which he or she has applied.

The high school counselor is crucial at this moment in your teen's academic career. Counselors can provide both consolation and realistic guidance. They can also make phone calls. A call to the most appropriate and reasonable college choice on a student's list can have positive results. Counselors can call several other schools, too, to find out where admission openings still exist. In late May or early June, the Independent Educational Consultants Association (IECA) and the regional Boards of Higher Education publish lists of colleges that still have admission spaces. A student, with his or her counselor's help, can explore these possibilities. (An independent counselor may also be worth the investment. Unlike the high school counselor, he or she isn't handling the entire junior class plus the scheduling for next year while trying to help your son or daughter.)

Your teen can still apply in a second round of applications to colleges with rolling admission. There are deadlines that have not passed—some schools accept applicants through June, and some large state universities accept students through the summer. In addition, some schools allow students who have not been accepted to take classes during the summer or on a part-time basis in the fall. Your teen's school of choice may offer this option. If so, your teen may want to take advantage of the opportunity to establish a track record at the college. Then, with good grades, he or she may reapply and be accepted (with credit for courses already taken).

Finally, there are many year-off options. Colleges expect

a percentage of their applicants to be "stop-outs" who have taken a year off or who have participated in a special post–high school program such as Dynamy in Worcester, Massachusetts. Encouraging personal growth and self-confidence, Dynamy serves as a bridge between high school and college. It offers outdoor leadership experience, supervised apartment living, and internships in career areas. Apprenticeship programs are another possibility. They can take your teen into a lawyer's office in New York or off to coastal Maine to build boats. Your teen's college of choice may view an experience like this as a plus on next year's application. There are many European programs as well.

The important thing is to *stay calm*. Don't grasp at acceptance anywhere. Explore the options and choose the one that's best for your son or daughter.

As for John, he had applied to nothing but Ivy League schools, with his dad's alma mater as a fallback. After he had been rejected everywhere, he looked around, applied to the state school nearby with plans to transfer after a year, and then found out that there were a few highly selective colleges with places still open. His high grades and strong test scores ultimately took him to a top school, Emory, where he's thriving.

GEORGETOWN UNIVERSITY

> "What do colleges look for in transfer applicants? Do transfer applicants have a tougher time getting accepted than freshman applicants?"

Letitia W. Peterson
Associate Dean of Admission

When students apply for transfer admission, the tacit assumption is that they are not satisfied with their current college or university. Perhaps the college they originally chose was not a "good fit," or they may perceive that another college will allow them to pursue a program of study that is not available at their own institution. Hopefully, even though they intend to leave their school, they have taken advantage of all it has to offer because, ironically, the students most likely to be admitted as transfers are those who have been most successful in their previous college experience.

At Georgetown, the transfer admission process is very similar to the freshman admission process. Students select one of the five undergraduate programs, submit an application and supporting credentials, and are admitted or denied on the basis of a competitive review. Candidates are considered for admission to a relatively small number of spaces for enrollment in the fall following the freshman or sophomore year only. In 1987, approximately 20 percent of the transfer applicants were admitted out of a pool of 1,330. Because admission is competitive, Georgetown recommends that a student have a cumulative grade point average of 3.0 or better in previous college course work.

What process is used to decide admission, and what types of candidates gain acceptance? First of all, it is important to keep in mind that each undergraduate school at Georgetown has its own separate admission committee which is composed of a dean, faculty, admission officers, and students appointed by the Academic Council. Each committee member brings a different perspective to the selection process and examines credentials with a view toward how a candidate might perform academically at Georgetown, as well as how he or she might contribute to campus life.

The admission committee reviews both high school and college transcripts and standardized test scores (SAT or ACT scores are required; College Board Achievement Test scores are reviewed when available). The candidate's grades indicate both ability and motivation; course selection is also important. For instance, proficiency in a modern foreign language is an integral part of the curriculum in both the School of Languages and Linguistics and the School of Foreign Service. Therefore, the committee is particularly concerned with progress in that area. Difficulty of course work is a factor, too. Students should have challenged themselves in advanced courses or honors programs whenever possible. Generally, we prefer students who have followed a college curriculum that corresponds to requirements for Georgetown students at the same level. Although the strength of performance in college is most important, all things being equal, the committee often chooses to admit students who have shown consistency throughout their academic record.

Does this mean that the student who did not live up to his or her ability in high school but has suddenly blossomed in college is unlikely to be admitted? We emphasize that review is competitive, which means that the committee chooses those students who stand out compared to other applicants. However, the pool of transfers is much less homogeneous than the freshman pool, and committee members may be impressed by a spark of intellectual curiosity that the student developed after entering college. This is the area where the committee uses discretion to select candidates with the most to offer Georgetown. Many intangible, personal attributes surface in the application and may become as important as the academic credentials.

Through the admission of transfer applicants, Georgetown has the opportunity to enrich its mix of students. Our student body represents all fifty states, approximately one hundred foreign countries, and many ethnic and religious backgrounds. In an environment where 80 percent of the students live on campus, this diversity extends the learning process outside the classroom into the social setting. Therefore, members of the admission committee often put a premium on things that cannot be measured quantitatively. We scrutinize the required recommendations from deans and professors, looking for clues to the candidate's personality. Sometimes we can learn a lot from the reports of alumni interviewers. But in many cases, the student can make the greatest impression by the format and content of the application essay.

The candidate who can give us a glimpse of the adventures he or she encountered traveling by train through Europe for the summer, or who learned patience as a volunteer working with the elderly, or who overcame heat and monotony to earn tuition by painting houses can capture the imagination of the committee members through the application essay. There is no task so small or mundane that cannot be made significant by the effort and enthusiasm that went into it, and the impact of sharing its personal importance with the committee should not be underestimated. We look for students who can generate energy and commitment and who are able to communicate those qualities to others. These are the kinds of people who will add to the student community at Georgetown.

What is the profile of the typical transfer student who is admitted? Certainly someone with academic ability and personal character. But there is no common mold. Some transfers applied to Georgetown as freshmen and were denied admission or placed on a waiting list. Usually, the admission committee admires their persistence. Depending on what strengths they have developed at the college level, many are ultimately successful in gaining admission. It is not unusual for wait-list candidates to be admitted later as transfers if they have sustained or improved their performance.

Graduates of two-year colleges with a rigorous curriculum are logical candidates for transfer acceptance, since they have reached a point where they are ready to move on to a university setting. They often have family or financial circumstances that precluded attendance at a private, residential institution for four years. Recently, a young man was admitted who would have looked strong as a freshman applicant. However, both parents had died during his last three years of high school, and he had remained at a local community college in order to settle his family's estate. Other transfer candidates with spouses or children attended college intermittently but built up an impressive record. Although cases like these are few in number, the committee feels that such students add an unusual element of maturity to the student body and are likely to appreciate all that Georgetown has to offer them.

What advice would we give to a candidate who plans to apply for transfer admission? Treat the application process as seriously as you did the first time around. Even if you have applied to Georgetown previously (we will also examine the credentials from the earlier file), do not bypass any of the required steps. Definitely do not submit photocopies of old essays; rather, take advantage of the opportunity to write new ones. You have had a wealth of experiences since you left high school. This is the time to ponder what your goals are and how and why they've changed. Some part of the essay or application should account for your desire to transfer and should reflect ways that Georgetown will suit you better than your present situation does.

Go out of your way to have the optional interview with a Georgetown alumnus or alumna. It's the one chance you'll have to meet personally with someone who will submit a report for your file. Take along photography, artwork, an article you've written for a local newspaper, or anything else you're proud of having created. Often interview reports are the only shred of personal background we'll see, so be sure to talk about your family, where you've lived, or whatever will help the committee get a better picture of how you've arrived at this point in your life.

Most important, even if you're disappointed with your current college, make the most of it while you're there. You chose it; like it or not, it is the first building block in your academic career. If it has a great history department, take a few of the courses that interest you and try to get to know your professors. One reason you may prefer Georgetown is the attention you can get as an undergraduate; you don't have that luxury everywhere. But you will need a recommendation from a faculty member, and he or she should know you well enough to write something substantive. So make it a goal to develop a rapport with at least one professor. There's no sense in wasting a year of college life. Besides, you're setting a precedent for how you will approach the rest of your academic course work. Keep in mind the members of our admission committee and their perspectives. They like to see students challenge themselves. One faculty member this year was instantly attracted to a transfer applicant who was ultimately admitted by the committee. Why? The professor's recommendation for this student was glowing in its praise for her academic curiosity and potential. It made a particularly strong impact because the professor had been a colleague of our faculty member and was well respected in his field. A coincidence, maybe, but you really can't lose by putting forth the effort to learn and by becoming involved. At least, you will feel it was a year well spent. At best, who knows? You might be admitted to Georgetown.

Georgetown University is a four-year private university for men and women, located in Washington, D.C.

When Your Child's Favorite College Says No

Groucho Marx claimed he would never belong to a club that allowed him to be a member. Somehow the unattainable is always the most appealing; the available, by its very availability, lacks glamour. And so it can happen, and probably happens more often than not, that your teen has set his or her heart on a club he can't join, on a college that does not accept her. The thin envelope of denial from the college your child most wanted to attend is one of the first really potent rejections in life, and it hurts.

What do you say? Probably the less, the better. You can't protect your teen from friends' reactions. Only time will make things better. When you think about it, you both may have known all along that the rejection was coming. The favorite college was a long shot that good but not great SAT scores, a strong but not honors high school program, and an uninspired essay on the class play just couldn't quite reach.

Go easy on the sympathy and encouragement speeches. Like bandaids over major surgery, they just don't work. Perhaps talking on an adult-to-adult level about one of your own recent rejections—the promotion you didn't get, the layoff during a company takeover—will ease the pain. Remind your teen that the college admission staff didn't reject *him* or *her*. They rejected a folder, an academic résumé. If your child would like an explanation, encourage him or her to call the admission office at the college. An explanation may help your son or daughter understand—and accept—the rejection. But don't make the call yourself—and don't try to badger the admission staff into revising their decision.

As adults, we know the hardest lesson we have to learn and relearn is *perspective*. Perspective is power. We're not the job or the title we possess, or the house we own, or the car we drive. We're not the college we attend, either. If you haven't done so already, now is the time to teach your teen this lesson. By mastering it now, your son or daughter will be able to take a fresh look at the other colleges on his or her list, choose the best of the remaining alternatives, and go on to make the most of the experience.

As for the admission staff who said no? They just missed a great opportunity.

After Acceptance:
What Next?

"Be careful what you wish for—you might get it."

—ANONYMOUS

A realtor was showing a neighbor and her husband houses in a community near Manhattan. In one particularly overpriced and under-maintained house, the realtor praised as a major selling point the dining room's exquisite view of the New York City skyline. It *was* spectacular. Fortunately, however, both were aware that, though they might spend the first six months or so gazing out the window, the view would eventually begin to blend into the surroundings as much as the wallpaper or the rhododendrons. It would still be a bit of a thrill when guests came over and exclaimed, "Wow, look at that view!" but for its owners the house would soon be a matter of tax bills, a leaky roof, and the issue of how exactly to cut a very steep lawn.

There are similar forces at work in the business of college selection. Parents tend to see getting in as the critical issue and often overlook what it's going to be like once the child is there. Drive around a few high-powered college campuses and ask yourself if the privileged few who attend these schools feel they are as special on a day-to-day basis as they seemed in the abstract. It's fun when friends say, "Wow, your child goes to Harvard!" but the wisest of parents knows that teens who succeed in college have found something deeper than just the joy of having gotten in.

Many young people look upon the senior year as the preamble to all that is wonderful, liberated, and fun. Finally they'll be out of the house, free of their parents, and on their own. Their view of college is probably more correct today than it used to be. In the fifties and sixties, colleges still functioned *in loco parentis*, but by the midseventies most of that was swept away. College these days *is* the real world, not preparation for it.

Teenagers need to be aware that college is an ending as well as a beginning. When they go off to school, they will leave behind the comfort and coherence of family and friends. Relationships at home will never be quite the same again, and the old gang will drift apart. Without their usual support networks, teens may find the adjustment to college more difficult than they expected. After the first few weeks, many write home, "It's so different." It's supposed to be. By this stage in their lives, teens are ready for more responsibility and challenge than they ever had in high school. Ted Tuttle, the director of college guidance at the Wheeler School in Providence, Rhode Island, gives his seniors a stamp and a quarter when they depart. The stamp is for the letter home during freshman orientation: "Thank you, Mom and Dad, for all the sacrifices you've made so that I can be here. I love it." The quarter is for a phone call. If they have any complaints, they're to call *him*.

Parents themselves will have some trouble adjusting to the changes after their teen leaves for college. The end of the child's living at home is welcome in some ways. Junior's room may be turned into a den, a spare bedroom, or an office for Mom or Dad. But there is pain, also. Parents often talk about the departure of the first college-bound child in language similar to the words of mourning: "Things are different now that she's gone" or "I only miss him when I think about it, but I think about it all the time." Though it gets little attention, the period between acceptance and departure is tough for both parents and teenagers. During this time, they must prepare themselves for the most significant and difficult separation since kindergarten. Communication, as always, is vital. Talking with your teen about the changes you'll both be facing is a good idea.

Following are some thoughts from admission professionals on the academic and social adjustments your teen will have to make. Susan Murphy of Cornell answers the question "Is there life after April 15?" Michael Donahue of the University of Michigan talks about the academic transition from high school to college. Sheppard Shanley of Northwestern discusses some of the social adjustments your new freshman will have to make. And John Greene, director of student health at Vanderbilt University, offers some sound advice on how to help your son or daughter cope with college stress.

Now that your teen's been accepted into college, you've finished—and you've just begun!

CORNELL UNIVERSITY

"Is there life after April 15? What does our child do now that the waiting is over?"

Susan H. Murphy
Dean of Admission and Financial Aid

It's April 15. The college selection process is over, a school has been chosen, plans for next year are in place, and the pressure is off. Now what? Is there still a purpose to life after the final goal has been reached?

Absolutely! First of all, of course, your teen will want to complete high school in the same strong fashion that he or she began it. Why should your son jeopardize an academic career that he has worked so hard to achieve? Why should your daughter risk leaving high school in poor standing when she may need to call upon the school in the future? Beyond that, however, your teen may now want to head in new directions—directions that he or she has chosen, not those the colleges or someone else expects.

After April 15, your teen has a wonderful opportunity to build not only for the transcript but for the challenge. Many schools offer workshops or internships to second-semester seniors. An extracurricular activity, an unusual course, a different approach to learning, a research paper on a current author (with a phone call to the writer), or a work-

252

study option on a political campaign can ward off senior slump and keep those final weeks of school interesting.

Even if your teen's high school doesn't provide new challenges, the summer can be devoted to a job, volunteer work, an "exotic" course at the local university, a challenging personal reading list, or a new skill or sport to master before college.

Many of the school support systems drop away after April 15. Teachers "let go" of their seniors as graduation approaches, and counselors turn their attention to juniors. Meanwhile, much of the emotional preparation for college has yet to be completed. Psychologists call it separation anxiety; others label it the task of emancipation. Whatever the name, your teen is likely to exhibit some unusual behavior and to experience a whole new set of emotions as one chapter of his or her life closes and another opens.

Expect your son or daughter to start pulling away a little bit and spending more and more time with friends. It may be easier to say goodbye in the fall if the connections are not so tight and the feelings not so deep. Expect tempers to flare, too, when you start talking about redoing your teen's room or when a younger sibling tries to take over your teen's possessions (not to mention role) before he or she has even left. Be patient and supportive. Your teen needs the comfort and strength of family bonds now more than ever and will continue to need them as he or she heads off in new directions.

So much attention in senior year is directed toward the outcome of the college application process that it's easy to forget that there's life after the colleges have made their decisions. That time should be a period of growth and exploration as well as celebration for your teen. Help your son or daughter make the most of the exciting and bittersweet transition period between April 15 and "drop-off day."

Cornell University is a four-year private liberal arts university for men and women, located in Ithaca, New York.

UNIVERSITY OF MICHIGAN

> **"Now that our child has been accepted, what can we do to help ease the academic transition from high school to college?"**

Michael Donahue
Associate Director of Admission

The prospect of going off to college often causes students to doubt their academic abilities. They wonder how they'll finish all those reading assignments, write all those term papers, and pass all those comprehensive final exams. You can help ease the academic transition from high school to college by sharing—and discussing—with your teen this list of survival tips for the anxious freshman:

☐ As soon as you arrive on campus, put yourself on a schedule and stick to it. Time management is the most difficult task for new college students, and it can make or break an academic career early in the freshman year.

☐ Look upon college as a full-time job, and plan to devote forty to fifty hours a week to your studies. Although you'll probably be spending only fifteen hours a week in the classroom, your professors will expect you to spend an equal amount of time outside on your course work.

☐ Before you register for a class, find out as much as you can about it. Read the course description in the college catalog and any evaluations that may be on file in the counseling office. Talk to students who've taken the class. If possible, talk to the professor, too. Ask about exams and papers. Get a course outline and a reading list. Go to the bookstore and take a look at the required texts.

☐ Keep your own best times in mind when you schedule your classes. Early morning classes suit some people better than others.

☐ Try to achieve a balance in your schedule between reading courses and problem-solving courses. A typical college literature or history course will require a hundred or more pages of reading a week. A schedule of three or four such classes will quickly overwhelm the slow reader.

☐ Get your reading assignments done *before* you go to class. Your professors won't read to you from your textbooks. Instead, they'll emphasize certain points and develop others, provide background information, introduce related topics, present their own and others' opinions. If you get your reading done ahead of time, you'll understand the lectures better, you'll know what you do and do not have to take notes on, and you'll be able to ask questions about anything that confuses you.

☐ When you read, read *actively*. Either take notes or highlight key points in your text as you go along. You'll remember the material better, and you'll know what to review later on.

☐ If you're a slow writer or a poor note taker, invest in a small cassette recorder, and take it to lectures with you.

☐ Review lecture notes as soon as possible after class, while the material is still fresh in your mind. Fill in gaps that you didn't have time to fill in during class. If the notes are illegible, rewrite them. You'll reinforce what you've learned, and five days later you won't have to guess whether Manet or Monet was the father of Impressionism.

☐ Study in an area where you'll be free of unwanted distractions and interruptions. If you like a little background noise, your room at the dorm may be fine. If you need absolute silence, find a study room or go to the library.

❑ Develop a cooperative relationship with your roommate, and make a pact to be considerate of each other's needs.

❑ Use your study time efficiently. Tackle tough assignments and the subjects you like least first, while you're fresh; save easy assignments and the subjects you like best for last. If you need a break, take one, but keep it short. Physical exercise often helps: it takes your mind off your studies, relieves stress, and gives you a fresh burst of mental energy.

❑ If you're having trouble with a course, get help—as soon as possible. Don't wait until exam week. Tutors are available in most subjects. Ask your fellow students, check the bulletin boards around campus, or go see your professor.

❑ If you have a big project, such as a research paper, to do, break it down into steps that you can complete in an hour or two, an afternoon or an evening: check out the resources in the library, develop a bibliography, make a tentative outline, read and take notes on a chapter or an article. The important thing is to get started—and to keep at it. Little by little, you'll get it done.

❑ Don't study *all* the time. Have some fun, too.

❑ Finally, remember that many students before you have made the transition from high school to college successfully. You can do it, too!

University of Michigan is a four-year public university for men and women, located in Ann Arbor, Michigan.

NORTHWESTERN UNIVERSITY

"What social adjustments will our child face in college?"

F. Sheppard Shanley
Senior Associate Director of Admission

The great majority of college freshmen enroll in institutions either within their home state or in their local communities. Under 20 percent go more than five hundred miles from home. For college freshmen living at home, there is very little change in their social world. Some friends may leave for colleges far away, some may marry, and some may go into the military. But the surroundings are still familiar and so are many of the people. Whatever social transitions these students make will come later in college or afterward.

Students who do leave home usually have two choices of where to live as freshmen. They can take a space in one of the college's residence halls, or they can live off campus. Freshmen who live on campus will find themselves in a building variously called a dormitory, a house, a quad, or a residential college. Wherever they live, freshmen will be away from home among strangers all the same age.

College freshmen do not all behave in the same way, and their values may vary widely. Some students come from families with abundant extra money; others have paid for all the amenities of life out of their own wages. Some students come to college with deep religious faith, others with deep skepticism, and still others with near-total ignorance of or indifference toward formal religion. Students from various races and ethnic groups take very different views of how open American society is to them and how much a college education will alter their lives. Will it confirm or enhance their present position, or will it change their position completely? They may be headed well beyond what anyone in their family has ever attempted to achieve, either academically or professionally, or they may simply be living up to what everyone else in their family has done.

One of the historic purposes of going away to college has been to encounter just this sort of contrast in backgrounds and outlooks. Alexander Astin's widely known study *Four Critical Years* describes how most students change when they go away to college. Typically, they become more tolerant, less religious, and more liberal in their political views and social behavior. Students who do not like the prospect of changing probably should not go away to college immediately after high school.

What does living away at college really mean? What do freshmen normally face? Just how bad and how good can it be? How can a high school senior prepare for a new life? Let's consider some questions of basic survival. With no priority in mind, freshmen must eat, sleep, study, go to class, turn in their assignments, take tests. They must also manage their own money, perhaps not for the first time but usually in larger amounts than ever before. Many eighteen-year-olds can handle these responsibilities, and most even welcome them as timely challenges. After all, others before them have done all these things and more, and each year new freshmen feel they can, too.

Some students, however, cannot handle multiple responsibilities at the age of eighteen. They have never been on top of things or completely in charge before. Parents, teachers, older brothers and sisters, boyfriends and girlfriends have presided over one aspect of their lives or another. Freshmen who do not learn to cope flounder around, get bad grades, become discouraged, and may even flunk out. Or they may leave college before the ax falls, not quite sure what happened or why things went wrong.

One student I knew went to college with neither great drive nor habits of diligence. Bright enough, pretty good at intuitive and improvisational work, ambitious enough to want to be as successful as other people in his family, he nevertheless began to fall behind. He made friends, joined a fraternity, and had fun more regularly than his abilities or the surrounding culture would allow. As a result, he didn't get papers done on time, and he didn't study for examinations. Although he never actually flunked out, in the middle of his sophomore year, he left school. Without the habits of diligence and the skills that diligence fosters—and lacking the inclination to obtain them— he scuttled the first academic career he attempted. Fortunately, he found an alternative that worked and went on from there. He took a job for a year, then enrolled at a large public institution, where he stayed off and on for another three years. When he wasn't going to school, he worked. Eventually, at the age of twenty-four, he finished his bachelor's degree.

Not all students who leave home to go to college encounter the same challenges to survival that this young man encountered, but it helps to prepare for them. Students are less likely to drop out of college if they ask themselves some probing questions *before* they drop in: How hard do I want to work? How hard have I worked in the past? Do I really want to be around a lot of other people who are more able and just as ambitious as I am? If the answers to these questions are unflattering, students are well advised to rethink their plans. They may not be ready to enroll in a demanding academic environment.

Even students who are ready for the work face the challenge of adjusting to a completely new social environment—new people, new ideas, new values, new habits, new life-styles. They will quickly discover that their fellow freshmen differ in some very fundamental ways:

- *Honesty.* Some students are honest; others cheat and lie, even without knowing it.
- *Intimacy.* Some students like to pour out their thoughts and their feelings to their friends; others do not. Some use an invitation to intimacy as a prelude to manipulation.
- *Sex and sexuality.* Some students have considerable sexual experience before college, and some have none. Some have considered their own sexual orientation and that of others; many have not.
- *Social drugs.* Alcohol, cocaine, and marijuana are not unknown to high school students, but their use—and abuse—

varies greatly in the many cultures from which students come to college.

□ *Colloquial speech.* Some students are disturbed and offended by vulgar language and swearing; others never notice it.

Some students are comfortable with differences in these areas and are reluctant to pass judgment on fellow students who do not share their views. They see the use of drugs or the question of sexual preference, for instance, as a "live and let live" issue: "People should be left to lead their own lives. I know who I am and I'm happy with that." Other students, however, experience major difficulties in these areas and sometimes come to drastic decisions. One freshman was so upset when he found out that his roommate was gay that he transferred to a different school after a month. Another freshman listened for a whole term to what seemed like constant vulgarity and swearing. In addition, she saw widespread drunkenness. One weekend, she packed up and went home. Students can avoid such drastic decisions if they seek help as soon as an alarm sounds in a sensitive area. If they think their parents are too far away to understand, they can talk to a counselor, a professor, or even an older student.

What should high school seniors do to anticipate the kinds of social adjustments they'll have to make in college? First of all, they should be open to change. They should spend time in unfamiliar surroundings with people they don't usually associate with. They should do things they don't normally do—go to a football game, visit a museum, take a camping trip, attend an opera, volunteer at a soup kitchen. They should talk to people about "firsts"—first relationships, first jobs, even first kids—and find out how others have coped with them. Above all, they should talk to their friends. If their friends are going away to college, too, they'll no doubt discover that they all share the same concerns and fears.

Excitement is synonymous with going away from home for freshman year. Students are on their own, free to do almost anything. Difficulties do not necessarily lead to defeats. College just could be a wonderful experience.

Northwestern University is a four-year private university for men and women, located in Evanston, Illinois.

VANDERBILT UNIVERSITY

> ## "Our son is nervous about going to college. How can we help him cope with college stress?"

John W. Greene, M.D.
Director of Student Health

Freshmen face many challenges during their first year of college. Not only must they develop their intellects and achieve academically, but also they must establish their own identities and become more independent and self-reliant. Parents of freshmen have to deal with their own set of challenges during this time. Understanding the stress students face can help parents cope with change and support their sons and daughters during the college years.

The transition from high school and home life to college and campus life is the first major step in the transition from childhood to adulthood. As a part of this transition, students must learn to develop meaningful relationships with people other than their parents. Although physically separating from parents is growth producing, it nevertheless can be difficult. In fact, when students were asked to identify and rate the most difficult times during their freshman year, they identified the first month as the worst. Exams and semester break were second and third.

The "first month" experience is clearly related to moving from home to campus. Students have new living quarters, new friends (or the absence of old friends), new academic courses, and new competition to adjust to. Academic competition can be especially difficult. Many students who have always been near the top of their high school classes have trouble accepting the fact that they may not be able to maintain this competitive standing when placed with similarly ranked students. In a class of five hundred entering freshmen, it is not uncommon for 80 percent to have been in the top 10 percent of their high school graduating classes. Of course, it is mathematically impossible for more than fifty of those five hundred freshmen to be in the top 10 percent of their college class. This can be disappointing to both parents and students.

That exam time is stressful for college freshman is understandable—it's stressful for upperclassmen, too. But why semester break? In returning home for the first time, freshmen often find that they have to resume the child's role they left behind three months earlier. The same is true of Christmas break and the first summer home, two other periods that freshmen identified as stressful. When teenagers feel forced to take on roles they think they have outgrown, conflicts abound.

During scheduled holidays and school breaks, freshmen frequently make their own plans. They arrange to visit old friends from high school or to spend time with newer acquaintances from college, and they may resent any pressure their parents put on them to participate in family get-togethers. Expectations regarding curfew and morning wake-up time can also generate resentment. Freshmen, of course, have been able to set these times themselves at college, and they may view it as an intrusion when their parents attempt to regain control.

Parents can minimize the stress of school breaks and holidays by following these guidelines:

- ☐ Be flexible.
- ☐ Don't make plans that include your freshman without first consulting him or her.
- ☐ Expect differences of opinion and perception.
- ☐ Keep lines of communication open.
- ☐ Don't use guilt as a means of regaining control: "Well, I just can't believe that you wouldn't want to spend Thanks-

giving with your uncle. We had so very much looked forward to your coming home. But it's all right. We'll manage
somehow."
☐ Listen to your freshman. Most young people will keep you
informed if they feel they are heard.
☐ Enjoy your freshman as much as possible *without* using
break time primarily for "constructive criticism."

In addition to dealing with stress, freshmen must learn specific
coping skills. At the end of their first year of college, students were
asked to identify and rate the tasks most difficult to master. The top
five, ranked in order of difficulty, were (1) managing time, (2) coping
with stress and competition, (3) making friends and overcoming lone-
liness, (4) resolving conflicts, and (5) meeting academic obligations.
Parents should note that academics finished *last*. When asked about
the order in which areas were ranked, students often responded, "If
I manage my time, deal with stress, have supportive friends and
family, and am able to resolve conflicts, academics are no problem."

Parents are clearly a part of the support system students need.
However, support does not mean prodding, instructing, pitying, or
giving gratuitous advice. It means being there, listening, serving as
a role model, and occasionally giving advice—when asked. Parents
should remember that the goal of effective child rearing is to lose a
child and to gain a young adult friend.

*Vanderbilt University is a four-year private university for men and women,
located in Nashville, Tennessee.*

Congratulations! Your Child Is Going to College

"Hitch your wagon to a star!"

—RALPH WALDO EMERSON

The blessing and curse about advice is that you can take it or leave it. It gives you a lot to mull over and pick apart, but it rarely fits exactly. Now that you've read fifty different views about college selection and admission, figured out what made sense for your own situation, and given your child the attention, wisdom, and love that made getting into college and getting ready to attend possible, we want to congratulate you. Nobody said the process would be easy, but probably nobody told you how difficult it would be, either!

For some parents and students, the process of college selection is more difficult than for others, not so much because of application forms and deadlines, but because of attitudes. Throughout our discussions with the admission directors who contributed to this book, we heard several points being made again and again:

❏ *Clearly the admission directors agree that an early start helps.* Students who are first-generation college applicants need to know that college is an option in the middle school years and plan their program accordingly. Students who have always expected to go to college need to follow the steps Alberta Meyer outlines in her "calendar" of preparation. Ideally, parents have already considered the financial burden of college; information on financial aid options is available in high school guidance offices and at the local library.

❑ *The admission directors tell applicants, "Be yourself."* This advice is not as easy as it sounds for most teens to follow, since their selves aren't fully formed as yet. For example, the college application essay that asks for a "shaping" experience or a significant influence can be overwhelming for some young people. If they don't see themselves as having a "shape" yet—a plan, direction, or even a set of prominent characteristics—this is a challenging question. Nevertheless, it is foolish for students to represent themselves as anything other than what they are. As Leon Washington says, admission committees aren't idiosyncratic cabals in search of the obscure; they're regular people looking for a good, strong, diverse class. No one gets in just on Dad's alumni connections or just on the essay. It takes a whole constellation of qualifications.

❑ *The admission directors know that students who use a "beat the system" approach to college entrance tests and their high school course selection usually try to beat the system in college and later in work.* Like the student in Chapter 3 who had one story for the admission committee at Scripps and another for the one at Boston University, some students try to beat the SAT, the course requirements, the college admission committee, the career guidance officer, and, ultimately, the company personnel office and employer. Because the high school record is the most important piece of information your child has to offer an admission committee, it should be a convincing picture of four years of intense effort, not "creative avoidance."

❑ *The admission directors caution students against using the application essay and the interview to "package" themselves.* The best advice your child can follow for the application essay and the interview is to write or talk about what he or she truly cares about; the reader or listener will sense the enthusiasm. Philip Smith warns against seeing the application as a "sales job." In the end, conviction and sincerity tell. Your child's abilities, talents, and interests should yield a choice of several schools to attend.

❑ *The admission directors encourage parents and students to remember who's in charge.* Students sometimes default on the college selection process because they feel like victims. They're daunted by the pressure and anxiety, and they're convinced they're not going to get in anywhere "good." As Nancy Donehower says, you and your child have much more power than you realize—not necessarily to get into Harvard, although those who do also have the power to choose among many fine schools. Even in the next ranks of excellence, however, there are many options. Don't set your heart on a single school for your son or daughter.

❑ *Finally, the admission directors wisely counsel: When it's all over but the shouting, remember that it's not all over.* Susan Murphy assures us that there is life after April 15. And your child's English, history, math, language, science, and gym teachers all agree. Don't allow the excitement of the upcoming change to spoil what's left of high school for your teen.

Talking with the admission directors prompted us to spend some time trading stories about our own college experiences, beyond acceptance and enrollment. Although we laughed at some of the memories—the "all-nighters" and the "mystery meat"—we recognized that we both established some patterns of behavior during those four years that we still rely on:

❑ We developed discipline—by going to classes on time, by studying most nights, not just before exams, and by meeting course deadlines.

❑ We took academic risks—by electing to take courses that weren't "easy A" fillers for program requirements.

❑ We confronted our books, professors, and ourselves—by learning that they didn't know it all and neither did we.

Your teen will establish similar patterns, and they will serve him or her well after graduation. But the love of learning will be the most help. In the world of work, it will eliminate boredom, promote sanity, and be the spark that others gravitate toward. Being interested in and liking what he or she does will make your teen good at it.

After recalling our college experiences, we remembered our parents and how they had made those intellectually and emotionally stimulating days possible—the financial investment, the letters and phone calls, the care packages, the rides home, the praise and support, the personal sacrifices. At the time we were more appreciative of the care packages than the other things, and perhaps your teen will be, too. If not now, the gratitude will come later. Meanwhile, besides the two of us, there are hundreds of educators, thousands of seniors, and countless parents who know you've performed a major feat these past several months, and they want to congratulate you.

FINALLY, your child is going to college!

Parents' Questions Update

Parents, we talked to many of you to gather the queries the admission directors tackle in this edition. But these can't be the only questions you and your spouses, friends, neighbors, and colleagues ask each other when you talk about your teens and college.

For a future edition, we want to know the questions we missed, the ones you personally would have put to the admission directors if you'd had the chance. If your first teen is going off to college this year, these new questions may help your younger children with their college plans. If you don't have younger college-bound children, the questions may help the people you know who do.

❏ I would ask admission directors:

_____

_____

_____

_____

❏ I want these college topics presented in the next edition:

_____

_____

_____

_____

Name _____   Mail to: S. MacGowan
                                             430 West 24th Street, #3F
Address _____   New York, NY 10011

_____

269